3rd Edition

Upper Intermediate

MARKET LEADER

Business English Practice File

John Rogers

	LANGUAGE WORK			TALK BUSINESS	
	VOCABULARY	**LANGUAGE REVIEW**	**WRITING**	**SOUND WORK**	**SURVIVAL BUSINESS ENGLISH**
UNIT 1 COMMUNICATION *page 4 /page 54*	Good communicators Collocations with *say* and *tell*	Idioms	Linking ideas An email	**Individual sounds:** Contrasting /ɪ/ and /iː/ **Connected speech:** Contracted forms **Stress and intonation:** Questions	Telephoning
UNIT 2 INTERNATIONAL MARKETING *page 8 /page 56*	Marketing word partnerships	Noun compounds and noun phrases	Linking ideas A marketing letter	**Individual sounds:** The letter *o* **Connected speech:** Noun phrases **Stress and intonation:** Noun compounds	Brainstorming
UNIT 3 BUILDING RELATIONSHIPS *page 12 /page 58*	Describing relations	Multi-word verbs	Linking ideas	**Individual sounds:** The /ɪ/ sound **Connected speech:** *Do /did /could /would you...?*	First-time conversation
UNIT 4 SUCCESS *page 16 /page 60*	Collocations Prefixes Idioms relating to success	Present and past tenses	Editing Negotiating	**Individual sounds:** The *-ed* ending **Stress and intonation:** Correcting information	Say more than *yes* or *no*
UNIT 5 JOB SATISFACTION *page 20 /page 62*	Multi-choice cloze: *Herzberg's theory of job satisfaction*	Passives	Editing Responding to job applications Linking ideas	**Connected speech:** Passives Stress patterns The *schwa* sound **Stress and intonation:** Lists	Cold-calling
UNIT 6 RISK *page 24 /page 64*	Describing risk Collocations with *risk*	Adverbs of degree	Linking ideas Describing events	**Individual sounds:** Consonant groups **Connected speech:** Consonant-vowel links **Stress and intonation:** Stress patterns	Agreeing and disagreeing Accepting or declining invitations

THE SOUNDS OF ENGLISH: *page 52*	**USING A DICTIONARY:** *page 53*	**SOUNDS AND SPELLING:** *page 53*

UNIT 1 Communication

A **Complete each sentence with the best word.**

1 Good presenters rarely ramble. They usually try to be as …*succinct*… as possible.

    a) inarticulate   **b)** hesitant   **c)** (succinct)

2 Her arguments were so ………………… that we all agreed to her proposal.

    a) fluent   **b)** extrovert   **c)** persuasive

3 The audience were very ………………… and carried him through his difficult presentation.

    a) responsive   **b)** eloquent   **c)** coherent

4 She is a very ………………… person. She always keeps her attention fixed on what she wants to achieve.

    a) sensitive   **b)** focused   **c)** fluent

5 He never says what he thinks or shows what he feels. How can anybody be so …………………?

    a) rambling   **b)** fluent   **c)** reserved

6 Everybody seems so ………………… here. They behave and speak freely, and do not really care what other people think.

    a) incoherent   **b)** articulate   **c)** uninhibited

7 We know that not all politicians are ………………… Some of them even use an autocue.

    a) eloquent   **b)** inhibited   **c)** hesitant

B **Match these words to make compounds and collocations relating to communication.**

1	extensive		**a)**	accuracy
2	eye		**b)**	communication
3	body		**c)**	contact
4	grammatical		**d)**	humour
5	sense of		**e)**	language
6	effective		**f)**	vocabulary

C **Complete the following phrases with *say* or *tell* as appropriate.**

1 ……*tell*…… a story

2 ………………… the time

3 as far as I can …………………

4 ………………… yes or no

5 ………………… somebody to do something

6 ………………… somebody what to do

7 ………………… hello / goodbye

8 ………………… a lie / lies

9 ………………… what you mean

10 ………………… something under your breath

D **Complete the following sentences with the appropriate form of *say* or *tell*.**

1 Can you think of situations when it might be better not to ......*tell*....... the truth?

2 How easy or how difficult do you find it to .... other people to do things for you?

3 In meetings, how often do you .... what you think?

4 Have you ever .... a joke in English?

5 How easy or how difficult is it to .... the difference between the banknotes used in your country?

6 Can you .... 'How are you?' in more than three languages?

7 When you were a child, did you use to do as you were .... ?

Check your answers in the key. Then answer the questions for yourself.

LANGUAGE REVIEW

Idioms

A **Complete the idioms in the sentences below with the correct nouns.**

1 They sent us a very long reply with all the details. But to put it in a ...*nutshell*...., that's it, we've won the contract!

2 I wish my boss would stop beating about the .... and tell me clearly whether or not I stand a chance of being promoted soon.

3 She expected profit figures and I was going on about sales figures. Once again, we were just talking at cross ....

4 Not official yet, but it seems we're going to relocate. Just heard it on the
....

5 If you think you can give a good presentation just because you know your subject inside out, well, I'm afraid you've got the wrong .... of the
....

6 This is a very badly written report. I just can't make .... or
.... of it.

7 I've tried to tell my boss, but it's like talking to a .... No reaction!

B **Reorder the words to make idioms.**

1 to / the / in / loop / someone / keep

2 to / straight / the / get / mouth / it / horse's / from

3 to / point / come / the / straight / to

4 to / picture / somebody / the / in / put

5 to / on / wavelength / same / be / the

C **Complete the sentences with the correct form of an idiom from exercise B.**

1 I know you couldn't attend the meeting, so here's a summary of the main points just to ...*put you in the picture*....

2 Let me .... : I think your performance is totally unsatisfactory.

3 I want to be .... I don't want important decisions to be taken without me.

4 I thought it was a rumour, but today I .... Andrew told me he was resigning.

5 Fortunately Sue and I .... so we hardly ever disagree about anything.

D Match these new idioms with their definitions.

1 air your views

2 be at a loss for words

3 drop a hint

4 give somebody the low-down

5 keep somebody up to date

a) tell somebody all the information they want or need to know

b) unable to say anything because something surprising or totally unexpected has happened

c) express your opinions about something in public

d) give somebody regular information about things

e) make a suggestion in an indirect way

E Complete the sentences with the appropriate form of an idiom from exercise D.

1 E-mail me every day to ..*keep me up to date*.. with the latest developments, will you?

2 When she was told she'd been nominated Businesswoman of the Year, she ....

3 Could you briefly .... on their financial situation before our meeting this afternoon?

4 Every week in our department there's a meeting where the administrative staff can .... and discuss problems.

5 We can't be sure, but management .... that there might be redundancies.

WRITING

Linking ideas

A Study the examples of linking words.

1 *Despite* his great sense of humour, he often finds it difficult to respond to his audience.

2 *In spite of* his shyness, he is a brilliant speaker.

3 *Although* he generally communicates his ideas clearly, I often find it hard to follow him.

4 *Even though* I'd put them in the picture, they didn't seem to grasp what I was on about.

Cross out the two explanations which are not correct.

The words in *italics* are used to

a) express the cause of something, the reason for something.

b) reinforce an idea, add information.

c) contrast ideas.

B Tick the three sentences which make sense. Then check your answers in the key.

1 I managed to follow their conversation, *although* my attention had drifted away. ✓

2 *Even though* the talk was awfully boring, I left the room after a couple of minutes.

3 *Despite* the fact that he knew he was right, he refused to admit it.

4 *In spite of* their criticisms, I didn't lose my confidence.

5 I was unable to express my disagreement *although* I am generally assertive.

6 I felt sleepy throughout the meeting *in spite* of my tiredness.

C Rewrite the three incorrect sentences in exercise B.

D Use your knowledge of linkers to guess the meaning of the words and phrases in *italics*.

1 Although Sue is usually very direct, this time she was really *beating about the bush*.

2 Despite the market's *bearish* trend, he was optimistic about share prices going up again soon.

3 Although he often tends to *waffle*, today he made a presentation that was clear, concise and to the point.

4 Their new product sold quite well even though the advertising campaign was a complete *flop*.

5 They managed to find a huge site for the new factory in spite of the *scarcity* of land in that part of the country.

An e-mail

E You work in the Human Resources Department of a modern, forward-looking organisation. You are very interested in the course advertised below.

BRENTFORD COLLEGE
BUSINESS AND ADMINISTRATION TRAINING
Autumn–Winter Courses

Communication & People Skills [Course Ref. No. 23-D]

The aims of this residential one-week seminar are to:

- improve participants' speaking and listening skills
- analyse common communication problems and explore ways of resolving them
- give participants opportunities to experiment with conflict resolution strategies
- help participants deal with defensiveness and aggressiveness.

This seminar will be of interest to all professionals who have to deal with people and work out problems with others.

Facilitator: **Kate McGovern**, PhD, MBA, President of Schröders Consultants in Geneva, author of the bestseller *How to Listen to Others and Resolve Conflicts*

Course fee (including manual): £650

Dates: 7–13 October

Venue: Brentford College

For further details, contact: Martin Lowles, BATP Brentford College, 27 Burrard Street, Brentford TW9 0AK
Email: mlowles@BATP.ac.uk

Write an e-mail (70–80 words) to your Head of Department, including:

- a request to go on the course
- why you think the course would be useful
- some details of the course
- an enquiry about the possibility of financial support towards the course fee.

To:	
Subject:	

International marketing

VOCABULARY

A Match a word from box A with a word from box B to complete the sentences below.

A	B
competitive	segmentation
product	retention
marketing	portfolio
market	strategy
customer	identity
brand	advantage

1 In order to secure a …*competitive*… …*advantage*…, companies will try to make their products and services stand out from their competitors'.

2 The company's aggressive ………………… ………………… targets numerous trade fairs around the world.

3 The CEO described industrial services as one of the three main growth drivers for Siemens, alongside its green ………………… ………………… and sales in emerging markets such as China, India, Brazil and the Middle East.

4 A survey by a German car magazine showed that customers were worried that mass market carmaker VW could damage the Porsche ………………… ………………… .

5 By '………………… …………………', we mean the process of defining and subdividing a large homogeneous market into clearly identifiable segments having similar needs, wants or characteristics.

6 The key to success is not in just securing the first order, but in fixing problems and offering new services. So we reward our sales staff for ………………… ………………… rather than just for the initial sale.

B Complete each space in the article with the best word (*a*, *b*, *c* or *d*).

To create the right marketing ……*mix*……[1], businesses have to meet a number of conditions.

First of all, the product has to have the right …………………[2]. For example, it must look good and work well. Secondly, the …………………[3] must be right. If you hope to make a good profit, you want consumers to buy in large numbers.

Then, the goods must be in the right place at the right time, so you have to make sure that the goods arrive when and where they are wanted. To this end, accessing the right …………………[4] channels is crucial.

Finally, the …………………[5] group needs to be made aware of the existence and availability of the product through …………………[6]. So you need to decide where and when you can get across your marketing messages to your target market. Besides, you also need to ask yourself how you will reach your …………………[7]. For example, you can get your marketing …………………[8] across by advertising in the press, on TV, on the Internet or on billboards.

1	a) strategy	b) plan	c) mix	d) profile
2	a) portfolio	b) features	c) extension	d) base
3	a) retail	b) identity	c) wholesale	d) price
4	a) distribution	b) exporter	c) survey	d) focus
5	a) USP	b) target	c) SWOT	d) wholesaler
6	a) discount	b) sample	c) promotion	d) questionnaire
7	a) profile	b) audience	c) strategy	d) retailer
8	a) plans	b) offers	c) samples	d) messages

LANGUAGE REVIEW

Noun compounds and noun phrases

A The words in each of the noun phrases below are in the wrong order. Write the phrases in their correct form.

1 report confidential marketing highly *highly confidential marketing report*

2 balance improving sheet steadily ....

3 research market ambitious programme ....

4 relations new department public ....

5 figures impressive profit extremely ....

6 operations rapidly overseas expanding ....

B Find the word which can make a compound or a collocation with both words on the left and both words on the right, as in the example. The number of dashes corresponds to the number of missing letters.

	Left words			Right words
1	target youth	m *arket*	m *arket*	segmentation share
2	niche global	m _ _ _ _ _ _ _	m _ _ _ _ _ _ _	campaign budget
3	fair world	t _ _ _ _	t _ _ _ _	fair deficit
4	outdoor Internet	a _ _ _ _ _ _ _ _	a _ _ _ _ _ _ _ _	campaign agency
5	premium leading	b _ _ _ _	b _ _ _ _	image name
6	car overseas	s _ _ _ _	s _ _ _ _	figures department

WRITING
Linking ideas

A Match the appropriate sentence halves below and join them with the correct linker.

1 The company is planning a direct mail campaign

2 Their mailing list contains plentiful information and data

3 Their competitors, however, still have to go through a specialist direct mail agency

4 Every company must work hard

5 The government decided to introduce a quota

6 They increased their competitiveness

in order to

with a view to

so that

compete or even survive.

improving sales of their range of office supplies.

limiting exports of textile products from India.

reach potential customers, which costs them extra time and money.

their market share would increase.

they won't have any difficulty identifying the most appropriate recipients for the mailshots.

B Cross out the two explanations which are not correct.

The three linkers in exercise A are used to

a) contrast ideas.

b) express the cause of something.

c) express the purpose of something.

C Read the passage below about international marketing.

In most of the lines **1–12** there is **one extra word** which does not fit. Some lines, however, are correct.

If a line is **correct**, put a tick (✓) on the appropriate line.

If there is an **extra word** in the line, write that word in the space provided.

Globalisation has affected marketing strategies in many ways. In the past, for example, how to enter a market tended to be the main question.

Today, by the contrast, international marketers ask themselves whether it is better 　 1 ....the........

to standardise or to adapt a product across different markets. Finding the right 　 2 ....✓........

international mix it has become one of the key questions, and answers vary greatly 　 3 ....

from a company to company and from product to product. Coca-Cola, for example, 　 4 ....

has customised its soft drinks to every market. It is well known fact that Coke in 　 5 ....

Indonesia tastes lot different from Coke in the UK. Such a strategy is in stark 　 6 ....

contrast to Rolex's. Indeed, Rolex uses the same advertising message, and positions 　 7 ....

its watches in the same way in the world over. Other companies strike a 　 8 ....

compromise between customising and standardising, and opt for a middle-of-the 　 9 ....

road strategy. Car manufacturers, for example, cannot afford them to design a 　 10 ....

separate car for each market. However, they do need to think of a country-specific 　 11 ....

differentiating features, as consumer tastes vary enormously from one country to 　 12 ....

another.

FT Publishing
FINANCIAL TIMES

A marketing letter

D The letter below was sent by an institute for management development to a large number of companies throughout Eastern and Central Europe. As you read it, complete it with the correct form of the verbs from the box.

> arrange   consider   contact   enclose   ~~forward~~   require

CENTRAL EUROPEAN INSTITUTE FOR MANAGEMENT DEVELOPMENT

Hviezdoslavovo nam. 128

812 03 Bratislava

20 June

Dear Sir or Madam

I have pleasure in enclosing five copies of our new brochure, detailing the Strategic Leadership Programme and the Advanced Management Programme available here at the Bratislava Central European Institute for Management Development for entry next September.

I should be grateful if you could please ...*forward*...[1] the brochure as appropriate within your organisation, so that it is available to both the Head of Human Resources and employees when ....[2] professional development options.

In addition, I ....[3] a poster which includes prepaid response cards and should be most grateful if you could ....[4] for this to be displayed.

Should you ....[5] further copies of either brochure or poster, please ....[6] Igor Cutka at our Admissions Office by email on I.Cutka3@pk.uniba.sk.

Finally, I hope you and your staff find the brochure of interest.

Yours faithfully

Irena Trollerova

Professor Irena Trollerova MBA

Head of the CEIMD

E Ivan Gasperlin, the manager of Kommerz Bank (Trubarjeva 47, 1000 Ljubljana, Slovenia) wishes to order five more copies of both the brochure and the poster. Write an e-mail message.

UNIT 3 Building relationships

VOCABULARY

A Study how Speaker B responds to what Speaker A says. Focus on the words in *italics*.

A: What do you think *damaged* our relations with Oxaco?

B: Well, I'd say communication problems certainly *soured* them a bit.

Speaker B doesn't repeat the same verb as Speaker A but instead uses a verb with a very similar meaning.

Now take Speaker B's part. Use the correct form of a verb from the box.

foster restore sever undermine strengthen build up

1 A: Their firm has *developed* considerably.

   B: Yeah. They've certainly managed to .... a good business over the years.

2 A: Getting rid of those trade barriers should *cement* the friendship between our countries.

   B: Absolutely. There's nothing like trade to .... relations.

3 A: It's good to hear that they're thinking of *resuming* diplomatic relations, isn't it?

   B: Yes. That's great. .... relations is probably the best decision.

4 A: The key question is, how can we *encourage* cooperation between our organisations?

   B: Definitely. We need to find ways to .... cooperation.

5 A: I'm afraid lack of communication is now *jeopardising* our relations.

   B: I agree. I think it's really .... future cooperation.

6 A: I hear Riel Engineering has *broken off* relations with its main distributor.

   B: To be honest, I wonder what took them so long to .... relations with such an unreliable distributor.

B Complete each sentence with the best word (*a*, *b* or *c*).

1 To do business with someone, first you should try to ..... *establish* ..... a rapport.

   a) improve   **b)** (establish)   **c)** promote

2 Their repeated interventions .... the whole meeting.

   a) corrupted   **b)** broke off   **c)** disrupted

3 Japan is trying to .... a much warmer relationship with China.

   a) cut off   **b)** improve   **c)** cultivate

4 China's desire to .... a solid relationship with the US has been the anchor of its foreign policy for several decades.

   a) maintain   **b)** undermine   **c)** strain

5 Thanks to its sponsorship of various cultural events, the company .... very good relations with the local community.

   a) resumes   **b)** enjoys   **c)** improves

6 With a view to fostering economic prosperity, the European Union has launched an initiative to .... closer relations with a number of ex-Soviet states.

   a) establish   **b)** disrupt   **c)** damage

LANGUAGE REVIEW

Multi-word verbs

A **Match these sentence halves.**

1 Jarvis will never let down

2 Sue and Marco are going to share a small office

3 In three years' time we plan to set up

4 I asked them to draw up

5 When we heard we'd lost the deal,

6 This conference is crucial

7 Tod's CEO expects China and India to account

8 We're looking for new ways

a) for as much as 25 per cent of revenues in the near future.

b) so we can't afford to put it off once again.

c) we called off the party immediately.

d) a customer who has a problem.

e) of strengthening our relations with our suppliers.

f) so they'd better learn to get on together.

g) the contract as soon as possible.

h) a distribution network in Mexico.

B **Complete each conversation with the correct form of a multi-word verb from the box.**

| count on | check in | go back | go over | look forward to |
| meet up | turn round | turn up | work out | carry on |

1 A: Do you think our new agent is reliable?

B: Absolutely. I know you can ..*count on*.. her to boost sales.

2 A: I'm really glad I'll be able to go to the Frankfurt conference.

B: Me, too. I'm very much .... seeing you there.

3 A: Those new models have really saved the factory from closure, haven't they?

B: Yeah. They've .... the company ....

4 A: Do you socialise with them?

B: Well, we usually .... for lunch on Thursdays.

5 A: The negotiation was a great success.

B: Yes. Things .... pretty well in the end.

6 A: Have you checked the report?

B: Yes. I .... it yesterday.

7 A: I suppose you all stood up when the CEO arrived.

B: No. In fact everyone .... working as if nothing had happened.

8 A: Hi Jeff. Igor here. Have you arrived at the hotel yet?

B: Hi Igor. Yes, I'm just .... now.

9 A: Was everyone on time?

B: Almost everyone. Hans .... late as usual.

10 A: Is *guanxi* an old concept, then?

B: Oh yes. It .... thousands of years.

A **Study these sentences, then decide whether the three statements below are true or false.**

WRITING
Linking ideas

- *Although* their prices are very competitive, we have decided not to do business with them.

- Their ads are hardly noticeable. *Nevertheless*, they keep attracting new customers.

a) *Although, even though, in spite of, despite, nevertheless, nonetheless, however, yet, on the other hand* are all used to **contrast** ideas.

b) *Although, even though, in spite of, despite* are used to **link parts of a sentence together**.

c) *Nevertheless, nonetheless, however, yet, on the other hand* are used to **link ideas across sentences**.

B **Complete each sentence with the correct linker (*a*, *b* or *c*).**

1 Relations between the two countries seemed to improve ..*even though*.. they kept putting off the peace talks.

   a) however   **b)** (even though)   **c)** despite

2 Their prices are very competitive. ...., we have decided not to do business with them.

   a) Nonetheless   **b)** Although   **c)** Furthermore

3 We reached out to customers with special offers, continuity programmes and appreciation letters. ...., customer retention did not improve.

   a) However   **b)** Despite   **c)** Even though

4 Negotiating prices and securing orders is very exciting. ...., ensuring that the customer remains a customer can be less stimulating.

   a) Moreover   **b)** In spite of   **c)** On the other hand

5 He likes keeping himself to himself. .... he spends a lot of time entertaining suppliers.

   a) As well as   **b)** Besides   **c)** Yet

6 Tsampa and Rexon have only been doing business for a couple of months. ...., Tsampa's managers have already given Rexon their full confidence.

   a) Despite   **b)** Nevertheless   **c)** Besides

C **Read the passage below about giving presentations.**

In each line **1–8** there is **one wrong word**.

For each line, **underline the wrong word** in the text, and **write the correct word** in the space provided.

It is probably true that the most effective presenters have all developed their own special way of captivating their audience.

Having said that, they often have a number of common <u>feature</u>. Like all good   **1** ..*features*..

communicators, they are aware that there audience is just as important as what they   **2** ....

have to say. Therefore, they tried to find out how much their listeners already know   **3** ....

about the topic, and about their attitude for it. Whenever possible, good presenters   **4** ....

also arrive 10 or 15 minutes before their talking is due to start. This gives them   **5** ....

plenty of time not only to prepare their notes and check the equipments but also to   **6** ....

chat to the participants as they come in. By create a relaxed atmosphere, they can   **7** ....

easily establish rapport for the audience. And good rapport, as many presenters will   **8** ....

tell you, is half the battle.

D Read the direct marketing letter below and cross out the one sentence which does not fit in.

morrison office supplies international

1 Connaught Place, Edinburgh EH2 7EY
Tel/Fax 0131 123 7650

Mr F. Potter
Futuro Office
98 Artillery Lane, Harefield,
Uxbridge, Middlesex UB7 5LS
21 September

Dear Mr Potter,

Thank you for doing business with us for over three years.

We continue to be one of the world's leading business-to-business suppliers of office products and services, and our motto continues to be: 'Our job is to make your job easier'.

Now, be prepared to be surprised about our latest additions to our wide range of products:

- Morrison's combined PXL-100 Laser Copier / Printer / Scanner – it does what none of the competition is able to do in the same way
- our new collection of *Wizard* office chairs
- our recently expanded collection of *Avalon* seminar chairs.

For more information, call: 0800 123 9876 or visit our website: www.morrison.co.uk

You will notice that our site has been completely redesigned to provide you with more information, and to serve you better. Let us know what you think about it. The company runs other funds that would have competed with the joint venture. Register with our site by 1 October and win an ergonomic desk chair worth GBP300!

We would also like to draw your attention to our special offers for regular customers like you:

- up to 30% discount off the normal purchase price on ALL orders placed in October
- free consultations.

We look forward to continuing our business with you.

Best regards,

Frank Lindsey

Frank Lindsey, General Manager, Morrison UK

E You work for Futuro Office. Write a short reply (100–150 words) to Morrison Office Supplies International.

- Express interest in *one* of the three products mentioned in their letter, and request further information.
- Enquire about the exact discount for that particular product.
- Tell them what you think about their new website.

USEFUL LANGUAGE	
Thank you for your letter of ...	We would like to take this opportunity to ...
	Meanwhile, we would like to ...
Could you please let us have further details of ...	
Could you please specify ...	We look forward to hearing from you.
We would welcome more information about ...	We look forward to your letter.
As regards your ...	Yours sincerely,
Regarding your ...	Best regards,
With regard to your ...	Best wishes,

LANGUAGE WORK

UNIT 4 Success

A Match a word from box A with a word from box B to make the collocations needed to complete the sentences below.

A	B
global	spree
annual	crisis
business	recession
buying	point
economic	outlets
retail	sales
turning	acumen

1 Turkey is enjoying one of the region's strongest recoveries from the ...*global*... ...*crisis*... after suffering one of its sharpest recessions.

2 In recent years the airlines industry has suffered from terrorism, ... and rocketing oil prices.

3 Our company has combined .... of about $2.5bn with about $600m coming from Brazil.

4 Peak Sport Products, a family-run company that now ranks among China's best-known sportswear brands, now has more than 6,000 .... and is opening another three every day.

5 The acquisition of Rex Electronics marked a .... in our company's history.

6 The consumer electronics industry was leading the world out of recession by tempting consumers into a ....

7 While some fashion brands such as Burberry and Louis Vuitton have married vision with ...., all too often there is a tension between creativity and corporate finance.

B Add the correct prefix from the box to the words in *italics* in the sentences below.

~~over~~ co de ex mis out down re ultra under

1 The manager admitted he had ...*over*... *spent* massively on an IT suite the business did not in fact need.

2 Whether or not to .... *regulate* health care is a divisive issue in many countries.

3 When two of our .... -*workers* disappeared, all the boss had to say was that 'they'd left to pursue other opportunities'.

4 We design and manufacture .... -*efficient* air conditioners for industrial use.

5 The profit figures are excellent. Once again, we've .... *performed* all our rivals.

6 The .... -*president* of Lexton Steel Corporation is suing for $1.5 million he says the company owes him as a retirement payment.

7 Staff who never get any praise for their achievements may end up .... *rating* their own abilities.

8 In the late 1990s, many countries experienced a severe economic .... *turn*.

9 Our company is thinking of .... *locating* its headquarters from Antwerp to Bratislava.

10 Of course I can see now that Brian is an asset to our company, and I'm sorry I so badly .... *judged* him when he started working for us.

C **Match these sentence halves.**

VOCABULARY +

1 It's been a lot of hard work, but she	a) are getting there.
2 New employees are often anxious	b) that chief executives rise to the top.
3 At long last, their hard work and investment	c) when a new product does well.
4 What we are looking for is a candidate who can	d) his life was a success story.
5 It is partly by knowing what to delegate, and to whom,	e) seems to be really making a go of her dry-cleaning business.
6 The reorganisation of our business is not finished yet, but we	f) is beginning to bear fruit.
7 From farm boy to business tycoon –	g) get results and work well under pressure.
8 Both retailer and manufacturer benefit	h) to make their mark and impress their bosses.

Underline the eight idioms which express the idea of 'success'.

LANGUAGE REVIEW
Present and past tenses

A **Past simple or present perfect? For each of the sentences below, choose the correct ending.**

1 Rebecca has been with our organisation for five years

   a) and she did a great job.

   (b) and she is doing a great job.

2 His hard work really paid off –

   a) he was promoted to Chief Adviser a year later.

   b) he has been promoted to Chief Adviser.

3 There have been serious problems with the merger,

   a) but we proceeded with it anyway.

   b) but we have proceeded with it anyway.

4 The motor trade has been in the doldrums

   a) last year.

   b) all year.

5 She's been promoted

   a) because she's brought off that deal.

   b) while she was working as Head of R&D.

6 How long have you worked as Financial Adviser

   a) for your current employer?

   b) before you became Financial Director?

B <u>Underline</u> the correct verb form(s) in these two texts.

NEWS DIGEST

1 Four exchanges censured for anti-competitiveness

The Securities and Exchange Commission _said_ / _has said_[1] yesterday it _censured_ / _had censured_[2] four US options exchanges for allegedly engaging in anti-competitive practices and _ordered_ / _was ordering_[3] them collectively to spend $77m on surveillance and enforcement. Without admitting or denying the charges, the American Stock Exchange, Chicago Board Options Exchange, Pacific Exchange and Philadelphia Stock Exchange _agreed_ / _had agreed_[4] to settle with the SEC and the Justice Department, which _were probing_ / _have been probing_ / _had been probing_[5] options listing practices at the exchanges since last year.

2 Karsen names Liebke successor

Karsen, the Austrian derivatives exchange, _appointed_ / _has appointed_ / _had appointed_[1] Dieter Lahm to take over from Hans Liebke as chief executive. The appointment _was announced_ / _had been announced_[2] yesterday by Deutsche Börse, which _owns_ / _owned_[3] 50 per cent of Karsen, and _is seen_ / _was seen_[4] as a move by the exchange to develop a stronger international presence.

Mr Liebke, who _has announced_ / _had announced_[5] his resignation from Karsen the week before, _was appointed_ / _had been appointed_[6] to the Deutsche Börse board a few days ago.

C **Present perfect or past perfect? Complete the sentences with the correct form of the verb in brackets.**

1 They ...*had hoped*... to organise a reception for their visitors, but it didn't come off. *(hope)*

2 They say they .... a message, but there's definitely nothing on my answering machine. I .... several times already. *(leave) (check)*

3 The manager is very upset as he .... outvoted at the AGM. *(be)*

4 We .... always .... ahead of our rivals until 2003 when they outstripped us for the first time. *(be)*

5 The new XY3 tyre series .... really ...., but then they were all recalled after a spate of complaints. *(take off)*

6 She .... me the low-down on the merger, so I feel well prepared for the meeting. *(give)*

D **Complete the article with the verbs in brackets, using an appropriate past or present tense.**

ZARA ONLINE

Spanish retailer Inditex has only relatively recently given Zara customers the opportunity to buy garments online.

The roll-out of Zara's transactional website ....[1] (begin) in 2010 in Spain, the UK, Portugal, Italy, Germany and France – six countries that are among the most important of the company's 76 markets.

Of Inditex's eight store brands only one – housewares retailer Zara Home – ....[2] (sell) directly to internet users until then.

Asked about the company's late arrival to internet retailing, Pablo Isla, chief executive, ...[3] (say): "For us, 2010 was the right time to go online."

Some analysts venture that Mr Isla, who ....[4] (make) Inditex the world's largest apparel retailer by sales since taking the helm in 2005, ...[5] (want) to concentrate on Asian expansion and cost controls before turning to new sales formats.

With its focus on fashion-conscious teenagers and young people, Inditex ....[6] (use) the internet for many years to promote its various lines and is also popular on Facebook, where it has over 4.5m fans.

Its smartphone application, which ....[7] (launch) at the beginning of 2009, ...[8] (download) by over 2m people.

"The internet and the world of social networking are extraordinary channels of communication which fit perfectly with our group's philosophy," said Mr Isla.

Inditex, whose brands also ....[9] (include) Massimo Dutti and Pull and Bear, is at the vanguard of computerised ordering and dispatching systems: in each of its 4,700 stores, managers ....[10] (provide) daily updates on sales and taste trends.

However, Mr Isla said Zara, its flagship brand, ...[11] (wait) for online demand to build before launching into cyberspace.

1 ......*began*......

2 ....

3 ....

4 ....

5 ....

6 ....

7 ....

8 ....

9 ....

10 ....

11 ....

FT Publishing
FINANCIAL TIMES

WRITING

Editing

A **Read the excerpt below about the chances of success of executives sent abroad to work.**

In each line **1–9** there is **one wrong word**.

For each line, **underline the wrong word** in the text and **write the correct word** in the space provided.

UK companies have failed in the past to prepare their staff in key areas before sending them abroad. What's new is <u>what</u> they are	1 ......*that*......
starting to paying attention to it. Previously, the definition of a	2 ....
successful assignments was that the jobholder didn't quit early,	3 ....
but now companies are waking up on the fact that assignments	4 ....
are not necessarily succeed just because the person stays abroad	5 ....
for the allotted period. While 89 per cents of companies formally	6 ....
assessment a candidate's job skills prior to a foreign posting,	7 ....
less then half go through the same process for cultural suitability.	8 ....
Even few gauge whether the family will cope.	9 ....

Negotiating

B **Read the follow-up letter to a negotiation. Write Norman Furey's reply to Grand Computers.**

- reply before 5 April
- express thanks for letter and brochure
- confirm details, but highlight misunderstanding regarding discounts: you had agreed on 3% on both the PC and the LJP

Dear Mr Furey,

Further to our discussion of 15 March concerning your order for 12 of our Nexus 2K PCs and 8 Orion Plus laser-jet printers, I wish to summarise the details and confirm the terms of our agreement.

List price		Discounts	
Nexus 2K PC	£650 inc VAT	10+	3%
Orion Plus LJP	£250 inc VAT	∅	

Delivery: Within a week for orders placed before 5 April.
Payment: Banker's draft

May I remind you that our offer of an 8% discount on our Nexus 2K PC is still standing, should you decide to order in excess of 20 items.

In addition, we are now in a position to allow a 10% discount on our new Orion Super Plus LJP/ Scanner, about which a detailed brochure is enclosed.

We look forward to your order and to doing business with you again in future.

Best wishes,

Ben Jacobson, Sales Manager
Grand Computers

Job satisfaction

LANGUAGE WORK

A Complete each space in the article with the best word (*a, b, c* or *d*).

Herzberg's Theory of Job Satisfaction

Frederick Irving Herzberg (1923-2000) was a management professor at the University of Utah, known internationally for his work on helping companies understand how to motivate workers and increase productivity. He is known for his 'Motivation-Hygiene Theory'. According to Herzberg five factors increase job satisfaction and staff motivation to perform:

1 Achievement
i.e. a sense of ..*accomplishment*..[1] or pride whenever a demanding task is ....[2] out successfully. One way managers can contribute to this is by encouraging employees to set clear, realistic professional goals for themselves.

2 Recognition
i.e. the ....[3] of an individual's or group's efforts, or contributions.
For example, managers can highlight staff efforts and contributions in meetings. They can also give a genuinely positive performance ....[4], and devise a judicious system of ....[5] such as housing allowances or extra holidays.

3 Challenging Work
For work to be ....[6], there must be tasks that are challenging or motivating. Just as each individual prefers some tasks to others, each finds some tasks more challenging than others.

4 Responsibility
When staff feel responsible and ....[7] for their own work, and when they are somehow involved in the decision-making process, their job satisfaction increases.
Managers can gradually increase staff ....[8] and decision making as they gain expertise.

5 Growth and Development
Everyone needs to continue to develop personally and professionally on the job. When there are limited opportunities for ....[9] and development, motivation decreases. Employees may commit energy to other aspects of their personal lives, seek other employment, or ....[10] out.
Managers can advocate educational or special training ....[11] for staff, and encourage them to attend training programmes and conferences.

1	a) inspiration	b) remuneration	c) accomplishment	d) astonishment
2	a) carried	b) broken	c) brought	d) pulled
3	a) reward	b) congratulation	c) prize	d) acknowledgement
4	a) examination	b) evaluation	c) testing	d) interrogation
5	a) perks	b) commissions	c) praise	d) loyalty
6	a) satisfying	b) fulfilled	c) completed	d) retaining
7	a) mature	b) accountable	c) mindful	d) comfortable
8	a) dependence	b) autonomy	c) separateness	d) liberty
9	a) rise	b) increase	c) growth	d) raise
10	a) break	b) run	c) fire	d) burn
11	a) absence	b) period	c) leave	d) term

A Complete the sentences with the correct passive form of the verbs in brackets.

1 Future success ..*will be driven*.. by developing a workforce capable of challenging the status quo. *(drive)*

2 Over 600 people ....redundant last year. *(make)*

3 Our sister company's leave policy ....recently .... *(revise)*

4 An agreement ....currently .... *(negotiate)*

5 If Tom ....a pay rise earlier, he wouldn't have resigned. *(give)*

6 Some people argue that during an emergency, a tough style of leadership should .... *(use)*

B Write questions about the sentences in exercise A using the verbs in *italics*.

1 How ....*will future success be driven?* .... *drive*

2 How many .... *make*

3 Whose .... *revise*

4 What sort of .... *negotiate*

5 Would Tom have resigned .... *give*

6 When .... *use*

C Look at the list of preparations that have been done or still need to be done for a staff training seminar.

1	design seminar programme	✓	(last Tuesday)
2	send out seminar programme	✗	(tomorrow afternoon)
3	book conference room	✓	(earlier this morning)
4	order folders and note-pads	✓	(last week)
5	check PowerPoint equipment	✗	(next Monday)
6	book a room for trainer	✗	(by the end of the week)
7	inform local media	✓	(earlier this month)
8	plan social evening	✓	(at our last meeting)

Now look at these two exchanges between the seminar organiser and her personal assistant.

1 A: Has the seminar programme been designed?

  B: Yes, it has. It was designed last Tuesday.

2 A: Have the seminar programmes been sent out yet?

  B: No, I'm afraid that still needs to be done. I'll see to it tomorrow afternoon.

Write similar exchanges for the other items on the list.

D Like the passive, the expression *have/get something done* focuses on what happens and not on the doer of the action.

A: Is the photocopier working?
B: Yes. We *had* it *mended* yesterday.
(We didn't mend it ourselves. Somebody mended it for us.)

Complete the exchanges with the expression *have/get something done* and the verb in brackets.

1 A: This office looks rather shabby, doesn't it?

  B: I know. We're going to .... soon.   (*redecorate*)

2 A: They want a copy of the contract in German.

  B: Right. In that case, we'd better .... immediately.   (*translate*)

3 A: The video's on the blink again.

  B: We definitely need to ....   (*fix*)

4 A: Our fire alarm seems to have a will of its own, doesn't it?

  B: Yes. I think we should .... without delay.   (*service*)

5 A: 'm not sure the figures in this report are right.

  B: Well, why don't you .... ?   (*check*)

WRITING
Editing

 A All punctuation has been removed from the following job advertisement. Rewrite it with the correct punctuation. Some words will need to be capitalised.

> fairertrade ltd seeks an assistant project manager for 12 months on this project funded by the trust fund for kazakhstan and administered by the world bank the project which commenced in january this year aims to improve the capacity of kazakhstani communities to manage local government structures for the planning and implementation of local development initiatives through the project village level development councils have been established across the country through which small scale grant funds are being channelled

Responding to job applications

B Complete the letter with an appropriate passive form of the verbs from the box.

> appoint   issue   pay   set out

Mr Andrew Harris
77 Dunham Road
Bolton
Lancashire BL3 2FK

14 March

FairerTrade Ltd
Denzell House
5 Connaught Avenue
Congleton, Cheshire CW11 7TL
Tel: 01260 271289
Fax: 01260 271288

Dear Mr Harris,

Re: Assistant Project Manager, Kazakhstan

Further to your application for the above post, I am pleased to confirm that the Selection Board which met on 11 March recommended that you ....[1] to the above post, subject to medical clearance.

Your salary ....[2] at the rate of £25,000 per annum.
Other benefits ....[3] in the particulars of post attached.

I should be grateful if you could confirm in writing that you wish to take up the post by Wednesday 20 March.

The proposed start date is on 8 April and your contract, which is for a period of one year,.....................[4] after we receive written confirmation of your acceptance.

If you have any queries regarding the terms and conditions of service of the appointment in the meantime, please do not hesitate to contact me on the above number.

I look forward to hearing from you shortly.

Yours sincerely,

Karen Poulson

Karen Poulson, Recruitment Officer

C   **Write Andrew Harris's reply to Karen Poulson.**

USEFUL LANGUAGE
POLITE REQUESTS
I should be grateful if you could confirm in writing that.....................   We would be most grateful for your prompt answer.   Your prompt answer would be appreciated.   Your assistance would be welcomed.
ACCEPTING AN OFFER
I am delighted to have been selected.....................   I would like to confirm that I do wish to accept the post.
ENCLOSING DOCUMENTS
I enclose a copy of.....................   Please find enclosed.....................   As requested, I am enclosing.....................
OFFERING ASSISTANCE
If you have any queries, do not hesitate to contact me.   Should you require further assistance, please do not hesitate to contact us.   If you should require additional details, please write to me.

Linking ideas

D   **Complete each sentence with the best linker (a, b or c).**

1   ...*Since*... everybody is here, I suggest we get down to business.

   a) (Since)   **b)** Due to   **c)** Owing to

2   The introduction of our new model was delayed..................... production problems.

   a) owing to   **b)** because   **c)** for

3   The slow rise in profit figures is..................... our large investments in new machinery.

   a) because   **b)** since   **c)** due to

4   The band's second album didn't do very well,..................... their video was banned.

   a) owing to   **b)** as   **c)** so

5   The project manager's off sick,..................... there's little chance of achieving much this week.

   a) as   **b)** so   **c)** since

6   .... unforeseen circumstances, the CEO had to resign.

   a) As   **b)** Since   **c)** Owing to

E   **Cross out the two explanations which are not correct.**

The six correct linkers in exercise A are used to

a) contrast ideas.

b) express the cause of something.

c) reinforce an idea, add information.

LANGUAGE WORK

VOCABULARY **A** Use the clues to complete the crossword puzzle.

Across

4 If you .... something, you consider the good and bad aspects in order to reach a decision about it. (5, 2)

8 If you .... a risk, you get rid of it. (9)

10 If a risk is ...., it exists now, or will exist very soon, and it needs urgent action. (9)

Down

1 If a risk is ...., it is so unimportant that you can ignore it. (10)

2 If you .... a risk, you reduce the chance of a large loss by sharing its insurance with others, for example. (6)

3 A .... risk is possible or likely in the future. (9)

5 A .... risk is very big. (4).

6 If a risk is ...., it is very small indeed. (9)

7 If you .... a risk, you make a judgement about it based on the information that you have. (5)

9 A .... risk is not likely to happen. (6)

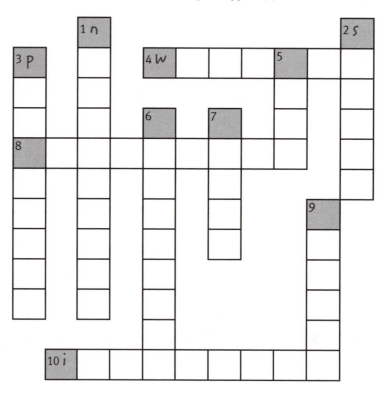

B Complete the verbs with the missing vowels. All the verbs collocate with risk(s).

1	2	3	4
_nt_c_p_t_	_nc__nt_r	_st_m_t_	pr__r_t_s_
f_r_s__	f_c_	m__s_r_	r_d_c_

C **Use these verbs to label the four groups in exercise B as appropriate.**

> *Assess   Meet   Manage   Predict*

VOCABULARY +

D **Match the following sentence halves.**

1   If the allegations against the CEO prove to be well-founded,

2   With such a provocative advertising campaign,

3   You can't hope to be successful in business if

4   I will say again that your complaint is unjustified,

5   If you play the stock market,

6   Try not to make a claim on your insurance policy this year, otherwise

a)   you never take a risk.

b)   at the risk of being repetitive.

c)   you risk losing your no-claims bonus.

d)   you should know you are doing so at your own risk.

e)   the future of the company is at risk.

f)   we run the risk of alienating our more conservative customers.

LANGUAGE REVIEW
Adverbs of degree

A **Look at the graph, which shows sales of soft drinks produced by Kanko. Then underline the correct adverbs (1–10) in the text.**

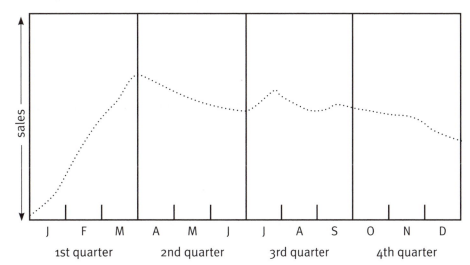

J F M A M J J A S O N D
1st quarter   2nd quarter   3rd quarter   4th quarter

As you can see from the graph, it has been a *rather/reasonably*[1] disappointing year for Kanko overall. However, the first quarter was *fully/exceptionally*[2] good, as sales of our new soft drink N-Ergy rose *steadily/dramatically*[3].
Unfortunately, owing to unexpected production problems, sales fell *sharply/steadily*[4] throughout the second quarter. They then rose *exceptionally/sharply*[5] until the end of July. The rest of the summer was *badly/slightly*[6] less successful, and sales did not pick up again until the first half of September. We were then *fairly/severely*[7] confident that we had the situation under control, but sales just levelled off throughout the next two months. Subsequent problems at our Norwich subsidiary, however, meant that sales began to drop *dramatically/gradually*[8], and there are no signs of a possible recovery at present. It appears that we had *moderately/badly*[9] misjudged the seriousness of the situation at Norwich, and that we were not *fully/fairly*[10] prepared to handle such a crisis.

B Complete each of the following sentences in such a way that it means the same as the sentence printed before it.

1 There has been a steady rise in sales since last winter.
Sales .... *have risen steadily since last winter* ....

2 The overall position shows a gradual increase in profit.
The overall position shows that profit will ....

3 They expected a dramatic increase in sales with the introduction of their new soft drink.
They expected sales ....

4 There was a significant growth in turnover, reflecting the group's rapid expansion over the last year.
Turnover ....

5 INO, the Swedish financial group, has announced a sharp rise in net profits to €1.14bn.
INO, the Swedish financial group, has announced that ....

6 Among electronics, there was a slight fall in microchip shares.
Among electronics, ...

WRITING
Linking ideas

A Study the following examples:

1 *Besides* organised crime and corruption, terrorism is also a grave cause of concern among executives.

2 The company is losing direction. *Furthermore*, its core products are losing appeal.

3 Sophisticated fraud *as well as* corruption and organised crime are seen as the driving factors behind the increase in risks.

4 Their financial situation is precarious. *Moreover*, there has been recent bad press about poor working conditions in their overseas factories.

5 There are financial risks involved *in addition to* legal and operational ones.

Cross out the two explanations which are not correct:

The words in *italics* are used to

a) reinforce an idea, add information.

b) contrast ideas.

c) express the cause of something, the reason for something.

Note: *furthermore* and *moreover* are *formal* words; they often occur *at the beginning* of a sentence.

B Match the following items. Notice how the linkers are used.

1 We need executives who can manage strategic risks properly

2 There are still very few investment opportunities in the region.

3 In order to increase our market share, we are considering a cut in our profit margin

4 What we need to do is always get up-to-date information about the risks we face

5 Increased competition is a threat to the survival of our company.

6 It is clear that the risk of civil war has decreased.

a) in addition to a reduction in all our prices.

b) Furthermore, we need to protect ourselves against negative changes in customer demand.

c) Moreover, the government appears to have the situation firmly under control.

d) as well as maintain good channels of communication between the key players in our company.

e) in addition to being able to take decisive action whenever necessary.

f) Besides, a political crisis is looming.

Editing **C** **Read this short text about health and safety in the workplace.**

In most of the lines **1–10** there is **one extra word** which does not fit. Some lines, however, are correct.

If a line is **correct**, put a tick (✓) on the appropriate line.

If there is an **extra word** in the line, write that word in the space provided.

Implementing a systematic approach to workplace safety will require	1 ....✓.......
for a cultural change in many organizations and within the safety	2 .....for.....
profession. All organizations they need to nurture a 'safety culture'.	3 ....
Company policy and workstation practice must dictate that safety	4 ....
never takes in a back seat to other interests. No one should	5 ....
be tolerate a potentially disabling or life-threatening risk in the	6 ....
name of cost-cutting, productivity or any other a priority.	7 ....
Safety and health considerations must be with an integral part of the	8 ....
operating policies of every organization. The consequences are too	9 ....
expensive when the health and safety are seen as secondary.	10 ....

Describing events **D** **Jeff Smithson, Staff Restaurant Manager at Kenko, talks to Paula, his assistant. Put the lines of the conversation in the correct order.**

...1... Paula: I hear someone had a nasty fall in the staff restaurant at lunch time.

.... A broken elbow, as well as a minor head injury. At least that's what Mary Dawson diagnosed. She called an ambulance straight away.

.... Apparently, one of our attendants had spilt some oil, and was about to clean up, but too late.

.... Jim Perry from Accounts?

.... Near the salad bar? But how did it happen?

.... Oh dear. Poor Jim! Is he badly hurt?

.... Oh yeah. She's got a first-aid certificate, hasn't she? It's really good to have someone like her around.

.... Pretty nasty, yes. You know Jim, don't you?

.... That's right, yes. Well, he slipped somewhere near the salad bar.

...10... Jeff: Absolutely. We need people like her. Besides, we must also make sure canteen users are properly warned of wet or greasy surfaces.

E **Use the information in exercise D to write Jeff Smithson's e-mail to the Human Resources Manager. Give details of Jim's accident (When/where/ how did it happen? Who is Mary Dawson? What did she do?)**

From:	JSmithson@kanko.co.uk
To:	MTPratt@kanko.co.uk
Subject:	Accident in restaurant - Jim Perry

Management styles

LANGUAGE WORK

VOCABULARY

A In the grid below, 11 words connected with *management qualities* or *styles* are hidden horizontally or vertically. One has been found for you. Find 10 more.

D	I	R	E	C	T	I	V	E	T	I	C
E	R	A	M	I	S	T	E	R	O	M	E
C	A	R	P	I	A	H	D	F	V	P	N
I	T	S	O	C	I	A	B	L	E	I	T
S	I	P	W	A	T	V	O	E	S	S	R
I	O	G	E	R	A	O	R	X	U	T	A
V	N	N	R	I	L	O	G	I	C	A	L
E	A	T	I	E	X	U	A	B	E	B	I
P	L	A	N	A	V	P	S	L	O	O	S
R	O	R	G	A	N	I	S	E	D	L	I
A	U	T	O	C	R	A	T	I	C	E	N
S	V	E	I	N	S	P	I	R	I	N	G

B Complete the table with the missing words.

	Adjective	Opposite	Noun form
1)	*sociable*	*unsociable*	sociability
2)	competent	....	....
3)	....	....	loyalty
4)	....	inconsiderate	....
5)	responsible	....	....
6)	decisive	....	....

C Complete each sentence with the most suitable word from exercise B.

1 Mark is not ...*unsociable*..., he just doesn't like hanging out in pubs after work.

2 He didn't know his job at all. The tasks were obviously not within his ....

3 Employees are free to look for, and accept, new jobs, but they must remain .... to their employers during the remainder of employment.

4 If Ryanair planes don't have reclining seats, it is not out of .... for long-legged customers, but to keep maintenance costs down.

5 It is extremely .... to accuse a country of being the source of cyber attacks prior to any serious investigation. The consequences could be disastrous.

6 What do you mean, 'Maybe yes'? Sometimes I wish you were more ....!

D Complete each space in the article with the best word (*a*, *b*, *c* or *d*).

EFFECTIVE LEADERSHIP

As we all know, effective leadership is hard to define and even harder to find. 'Like parenthood,' says a Harvard psychologist, 'leadership will never be an exact science. ....*However*................[1], research can help business leaders get a clearer ....[2] of what it takes to lead effectively, in the same way as it has helped parents in recent years.'

One may ....[3] to what extent such an analogy is helpful. In fact, research on parenting provides very ....[4] results, and there seems to be a theory to ....[5] every opinion. In the ....[6] though, the majority of parents work things out for themselves through a process of trial and ....[7].

But what about leadership? Different styles have been identified: democratic, coercive, coaching, authoritative, pacesetting, etc. A 'coercive' leader, for instance, would expect you to do as you were told, whereas a 'coaching' one might simply make a suggestion. ....[8] one is talking about parenting or leadership, the trick is of course to know which style to adopt when, and unfortunately research is not very useful in this respect. So it seems that for both parents and leaders, it is back to trial and error and ....[9] instinct.

1	**a)** Although	**b)** (However)	**c)** But	**d)** Despite
2	**a)** photo	**b)** picture	**c)** scene	**d)** sketch
3	**a)** imagine	**b)** criticise	**c)** think	**d)** wonder
4	**a)** contradictory	**b)** antagonistic	**c)** consistent	**d)** anticipated
5	**a)** adopt	**b)** suit	**c)** adapt	**d)** change
6	**a)** final	**b)** summary	**c)** conclusion	**d)** end
7	**a)** failure	**b)** fault	**c)** error	**d)** mistake
8	**a)** Whether	**b)** As	**c)** If	**d)** Since
9	**a)** gut	**b)** liver	**c)** stomach	**d)** heart

LANGUAGE REVIEW

Text reference

A Complete the sentences with words or phrases from the box. Use each item only once.

it   the latter   the one   their   theirs   then   ~~there~~   they   this

1 Pete knew he'd be late for the meeting. But he eventually got ...*there*..., - just to find out .... had been cancelled!

2 She wasn't sure whether to do her MBA at Burlington College or Durham Business School. Eventually she went for ...., as it has a distance learning option.

3 We want to allow our staff to do the job .... are paid to do. We're doing .... by using technology to take the administration out of people's jobs.

4 If staff want to order a new PC, they can select .... they like online, get .... manager to review it, and then send off the order to the supplier.

5 She became Commercial Manager only last September, but she already knew .... that she would be able to initiate some sweeping changes.

6 Our company seems too attached to traditional values, whereas .... has always been innovative and forward looking.

LANGUAGE WORK

B Indicate what the words in *italics* refer to in these two articles, as in the example.

1

Many multinational companies are desperate for managers with international experience. Is it possible that *they*[1] are ignoring the potential within *their*[2] own ranks?

Women in the United States account for 49 per cent of middle management ranks from *which*[3] expatriates are typically chosen. But *they*[4] make up only 13 per cent of US managers sent abroad.

A US organisation that seeks to promote women in business decided to study *the question*[5]. *Its*[6] report, published this week, says women are being held back by preconceptions about *their*[7] willingness to travel and about how other nationalities will react to *them*[8].

2

'Our firm runs leadership training courses for global companies and advises *them*[1] on how to develop *their*[2] executives', says Liz Cooper, a managing consultant at a leading recruitment and management consultancy. 'For example, if someone is not particularly good socially, *we*[3] would encourage the company to put *them*[4] into roles where *they*[5] are forced to work with people until *they*[6] get better at *it*[7] and so on.'

The answer to whether leaders are born or made is probably as elusive as the secret of happiness. But *that*[8] does not stop companies or *their*[9] employees trying to find *it*[10].

FT Publishing
FINANCIAL TIMES

WRITING

Linking ideas

A Complete each sentence with the best linker.

1 Our manager never shows any understanding if we let the work get on top of us and never encourages us. ....*Consequently*,.... we don't rate him very highly as a manager.

   a) In addition   **b)** Since   **c)** Consequently

2 Sales have been going down for over a year, ... a new policy is urgently required.

   a) as   **b)** although   **c)** so

3 Many staff were unhappy with the way they were being managed.

   .... , they were sent a questionnaire inviting them to assess their managers.

   a) As a result   **b)** Owing to   **c)** Besides

4 The different management styles within the team blended really well. .... , the project was completed to everybody's satisfaction.

   a) Therefore   **b)** Due to   **c)** Whereas

5 .... the project manager was off sick, there was little chance of achieving much that week.

   a) Consequently   **b)** As   **c)** In addition

6 The staff's high morale is .... the manager's empowering style.

   a) therefore   **b)** due to   **c)** owing to

B Cross out the two incorrect explanations.

The SIX correct linkers in exercise A are used to

a) reinforce an idea, add information.

b) contrast ideas.

c) express the cause or the result of something.

Letters of enquiry **C** **Read the letter of enquiry below and cross out the one sentence which does not fit in.**

TransChem Ltd
Dunakeszi út 127
H-1810 Budapest
Hungary

The Principal
Vernon Morgan College of English
11 Buccleuch Avenue
Edinburgh EH4 7BG

30 August

Dear Madam or Sir,

Our company is one of the leading suppliers of speciality chemicals to a wide range of industries in Eastern and Central Europe, where we have 12 branches. We therefore employ staff of many different nationalities.

With a view to increasing the efficiency of our operations, we wish to send a group of middle managers on executive language courses in the UK. We would like our staff not only to improve their communication skills, but also to further their knowledge of the kind of English needed in management and in the chemical industry.

One of our business colleagues has recommended your college as one of the best. Could you please let us have full details of your executive courses, such as term dates, fees and accommodation with host families. Good management looks after its existing clientele superbly and goes after markets offering the largest sales. Any other relevant details would be appreciated.

As we envisage sending 10 to 15 managers a year, we will naturally be looking for competitive offers and a lasting business relationship.

We look forward to your reply.

Yours faithfully,

Fekete Ferenc
Hungary Manager

D **Now write a suitable reply.**

* thank TransChem for their enquiry, and express interest
* briefly introduce the Vernon Morgan College of English (founded 20 years ago / high quality tailor-made language training for executives / etc.)
* mention the trainers and consultants (highly qualified / enthusiastic and professional / experienced in the field / etc.) and mention clients (AGROCHEM in Milan and Petrosur in Valencia)
* mention social programme (opportunity to mix with local business people)
* refer to enclosed prospectus
* offer 20% discount on course fees for first group (12% on subsequent groups – minimum of 10)
* close on an encouraging and optimistic note

UNIT 8 Team building

VOCABULARY

A **Make the following adjectives negative by adding the correct prefix. Mind your spelling!**

1	......*im*....... polite	6	.... experienced
2	.... relevant	7	.... imaginative
3	.... tolerant	8	.... enthusiastic
4	.... mature	9	.... practical
5	.... legible	10	.... efficient

Which two adjectives **cannot** be used to describe someone's character?

B **In each group, cross out the word which does not begin with a prefix.**

	a)	**b)**	**c)**
1	discontinue	disincentive	~~distinguished~~
2	miserable	mismanagement	misinform
3	biased	bimonthly	bilingual
4	reconnect	renowned	realign
5	prearranged	premium	prepaid
6	irrational	irreversible	irritable

C **Complete the sentences with the appropriate words remaining in exercise B.**

1 Mr Mozilo pointed out that the sales were part of a ...*prearranged*... programme, and not the result of week-to-week decisions that he made himself.

2 Executives who fail to meet the aspirations of their employees can be accused of ....

3 The new measures restrict employees' autonomy and will undoubtedly act as a ....

4 The move towards the creation of a shared vision is .... and lies at the heart of a people-centred strategy.

5 There will be some drastic changes in the way our company is organised. For example, we're going to .... all our marketing and sales activities.

6 Our project manager wants us to submit a detailed .... progress report. I don't really understand why we have to write reports so frequently.

VOCABULARY +
Fixed phrases

D **Correct any sentences in which the phrases in *italics* are in the wrong order.**

hard and fast

1 At the moment we have no ~~*fast and hard*~~ information about the reorganisation of Human Resources.

2 All negotiations typically involve a certain amount of *take and give*.

3 Many people believe that *wining and dining* helps strengthen a team.

4 It was still a bit *go and touch* whether they would push ahead with the plan.

5 The *pros and cons* of a thorough reorganisation have been discussed at length.

6 *By and large*, news of the reorganisation of the department was welcomed by the staff.

E **Complete the sentences with the correct phrase from the box.**

trial and error	supply and demand
rules and regulations	stocks and shares
peace and quiet	~~hustle and bustle~~

1 Our next People Skills seminar will be held in Martonfa, far from the ...*hustle and bustle*... of Budapest city centre.

2 The participants will enjoy the .... of the countryside after a hectic week.

3 This new economic theory proposes that the laws of .... are obsolete.

4 Some of the best teams are built after a painful process of ....

5 More and more people invest their savings in ....

6 The fact that he introduced so many .... upon his appointment did not make him very popular with staff.

LANGUAGE REVIEW
Modal perfect

A **Choose the best way to complete the exchanges below.**

1 A: The people in Accounts often say they can't work well together.

B: Well, we had a one-week seminar on team building last May. Maybe they

 a) had to attend it.

 b) must have attended it.

 c) should have attended it.

2 A: It is a pity Ron and Ken were always trying to settle their own personal disagreements.

B: I agree. I don't think the trainer

 a) may

 b) should } have spent so much time on such private matters.

 c) must

3 A: By the end of the seminar some people were still too shy to talk.

B: I noticed that, too. The trainer

 a) must have encouraged

 b) had to encourage } everyone to express themselves.

 c) might have encouraged

4 A: I particularly like the fact that we immediately had a clear sense of direction.

B: Yeah. But I thought the overall objective

 a) could

 b) must } have been clearer.

 c) will

5 A: One thing I wasn't too pleased about is how the trainer handled the argument about overtime.

B: Mm. How do you think she

 a) should have dealt

 b) had to deal } with that?

 c) must have dealt

B Complete these sentences in the best way.

1 a) Paul must have left the office early –   **1)** his briefcase is still here.

   b) Paul can't have left the office early –   **2)** I can't find him anywhere.

2 a) Ron can't have finished his report –   **1)** he's already working on another project.

   b) Ron must have finished his report –   **2)** he only started this morning.

3 a) You can't have deleted that file –   **1)** I have searched all the directories.

   b) You might have deleted that file –   **2)** all the files on this drive are read-only.

4 a) Sue and Ken must have had a row –   **1)** they hardly talk to each other any more.

   b) Sue and Ken may have had a row –   **2)** but that's not very likely, is it?

5 a) It must have been a tough seminar –   **1)** the trainer looked completely drained.

   b) It can't have been a tough seminar –   **2)** the participants were such nice people.

WRITING
Linking ideas

A Match these sentence halves.

1 If possible, do not delay, take action   **a)** *after* you have identified its real cause.

2 *Once* the aims of the session are clear to everyone,   **b)** *as soon as* you sense a conflict.

3 We'll have finished all the tasks   **c)** *before* you meet them all as a team.

4 It seems plain common sense to try and solve a conflict only   **d)** *by the time* the first team settle their differences.

5 Tim will plan the next seminar tomorrow   **e)** do encourage frank and open discussion.

6 It's a good idea to find out who each individual member is   **f)** *while* you write the report.

B Complete the sentences with the correct items from the box.

causal relations   time relations   purpose   past   present   future

1 We use the five linkers in *italics* in exercise A to express ....

2 Note that after those linkers, we use a .... tense to refer to the ....

C Read Jeff Bagley's e-mail to the Sales Manager, Ron Fox, about a senior member of the sales team.

From:	Jeff Bagley
To:	Ron Fox
Subject:	Confidential – Problems with sales staff

Ron,

What's all this fuss about Alan Carter? Every second day I hear someone complain about him for one reason or another. What's going on in the sales team? Could you investigate?

Find out what's wrong with him. See if you can put him back on track.

Keep me posted.

Jeff

Summarise the notes Ron took during his interviews with his staff to complete section 1 of the e-mail below.

- 'Why is he always late for meetings? We'd never get away with it!'
- 'Just because he has more experience, he thinks our ideas and suggestions are worth nothing.'
- 'I know my name sounds foreign, but that's no reason to tell me to 'go back to where I come from.' I'm so depressed I want to leave.'
- 'I'm finding it difficult to work with someone who's so arrogant.'
- 'A nice chap deep inside. Too direct, though. Some of us find him rude, even.'
- 'For him sales is a man's world and that sums it up.'
- 'If I missed half of each meeting like he does, I'd have time to make as many calls as he does.'
- 'He had the cheek to ask me why I wasn't at home looking after the kids.'
- 'He does not propose or suggest – he dictates.'

From:	Ron Fox
To:	Jeff Bagley
Subject:	Complaints about Alan Carter

Hi Jeff,

I had not realised that the problems with Alan had gone that far.
At your request, I have looked into the matter. First, I talked to his colleagues within the team, and then I had a long chat with him. Finally, on the basis of the information gathered, I drew some conclusions.

1 Feedback from the team members
The comments made by sales staff revolve around three areas:

a) ....
b) ....
c) ....

2 Feedback from Alan
When I talked to Alan, he admitted he was 'probably not the most tactful person on earth', especially with female colleagues, but insisted his attitude was mistaken for rudeness.

As regards his lack of punctuality, he explained he made more calls every day than anyone else, and that increasing sales, not attending meetings, was his priority.
Finally, he complained about what he called the 'aggressiveness and competitiveness' of the younger sales staff, and said he found it difficult to make himself heard in meetings.

3 Conclusions and recommendations
On the one hand, some of the complaints about Alan seem justified. In particular, he was reprimanded for his racist and sexist remarks and jokes. I have no doubt, however, that he is an asset to the department, and extremely committed to our company.

On the other hand, it is clear that there are problems within the team as a whole and that they need to learn to work together more effectively.
I would like to recommend that part of our budget be put aside for the whole sales team to attend the kind of team-building seminar admin staff attended last year.

Ron

Raising finance

VOCABULARY | **A** | **Complete each sentence with the best word from the box.**

mortgage administration assets ~~venture~~ business angel cash flow grants instalments overdraft stake bankruptcy principal

1 ...*Venture*... capital is a general term for money that is lent to someone when they start a business.

2 Customers not paying bills on time caused a major .... problem.

3 Repayment of the loan will be in ten .... at three-month intervals.

4 Surprisingly, BLT Inc. is selling off its 30% .... in Kommerz Bank.

5 The manager said it would be a disaster if the club were to be wound up rather than stay in ...., as the players would go out of contract.

6 The EU often awards development .... to its poorer members.

7 The .... is the original amount of a loan, excluding any interest.

8 We often reached our .... limit because of cash flow problems.

9 Their company has .... of £70 million and liabilities of £40 million.

10 They were in arrears with their ...., so their home was repossessed.

11 Unless the situation improves dramatically, our company will be forced to file for ....

12 We offered the .... a 10% share in the profits and a seat on the board of directors.

B | **Choose the best word (*a, b* or *c*) to complete each space in the article.**

Sources of finance

What do you need to consider when choosing the source of new business finance?

A key consideration is to strike a balance between ...*equity*...[1] and debt to ensure the funding structure suits the business.

The main differences between borrowed money (debt) and equity are that, with debt, bankers request ....[2] payments and capital repayments, and the borrowed money is usually secured on business assets or the personal assets of the ....[3] and/or directors. A bank also has the power to place a business into ....[4] or bankruptcy if it ....[5] on debt interest or repayments or its prospects decline.

In contrast, ...[6] investors take the risk of failure like other shareholders, whilst they will benefit from participation in increasing levels of ....[7] and on the eventual sale of their equity ....[8].

The overall objective in raising finance for a company is to avoid exposing the business to excessively high borrowings, but without unnecessarily diluting the ....[9] capital. This will ensure that the financial risk of the company is kept at an optimal level.

1	**a)**	stake	**b)**	equity	**c)**	capital
2	**a)**	interest	**b)**	loan	**c)**	cash flow
3	**a)**	creditors	**b)**	shareholders	**c)**	bankers
4	**a)**	registration	**b)**	accreditation	**c)**	administration
5	**a)**	depends	**b)**	deposits	**c)**	defaults
6	**a)**	equity	**b)**	stake	**c)**	venture
7	**a)**	assets	**b)**	profits	**c)**	funds
8	**a)**	mortgage	**b)**	loan	**c)**	stake
9	**a)**	share	**b)**	rate	**c)**	asset

LANGUAGE REVIEW

Dependent prepositions

A   **Indicate where the missing prepositions belong.**

1   The markets are suspicious ⎣ *a* the system's lack of transparency and banks have lost some of their influence ⎣ *b* corporations.

2   There is fierce competition in the growing market high-speed Internet access.

3   Some executives involved the deal argue that the competition authorities are intimidated by the complexity the issue.

4   They all agreed that weak management was largely to blame the downfall the company.

5   As the company had thrived rising property prices, so it suffered when they began to fall.

6   Public protests the cost of energy, as well as worries the impact business and inflation, are forcing governments to think hard about what their response should be.

a) of
b) over
c) for
d) in
e) of
f) for
g) of
h) on
i) about
j) about
k) on

B   **Complete the two texts with the prepositions given in the boxes.**

NEWS DIGEST

Kersta said yesterday it had entered ...*into*...[1] exclusive talks with Lindcom for the sale of Deltelfone.

Kersta acquired Deltelfone earlier in January and said then that it would dispose ....[2] the business.

Analysts say a flotation of 49.9 per cent of the business, which was scheduled ....[3] April if an agreement could not be reached ....[4] a trade sale, would probably have valued Deltelfone at 7–10bn euros. Kersta refused to comment ....[5] the size of the bid.

The takeover of Deltelfone by Lindcom would certainly create potential ....[6] rationalisation.

One of the largest carmakers is considering permanent reductions ....[7] list prices.

The proposal follows a spate of discounting by smaller rivals and the introduction of the government order aimed ....[8] opening up the new car market.

Executives are studying how such a price initiative would impact ....[9] its fleet customers, who benefit ....[10] discounts based on recommended retail prices.

Any cut ....[11] list prices would almost certainly force copycat action by other companies.

Carmakers have until December to comply ....[12] the government order on car pricing.

for	for	~~into~~	of	on	on

at	from	in	in	on	with

C **Insert the missing preposition in each sentence.**

1 Although the traditional approach had its strengths, it became an excuse ʌ*for* avoiding the structural reforms the country needed.

2 The engineering company KNG first hinted a share buyback last month.

3 Such buybacks are rarely implemented, although many companies have sought permission them.

4 The CEO said the company would concentrate medium-sized acquisitions.

5 KNG's international division accounts just 23% of sales.

6 Several governments insisted creating specific safeguard rules allowing them to block Chinese imports.

WRITING
Emphasising

A **Match these sentence halves.**

1 *Rarely* do banks agree	a) had requested a massive loan.
2 *Not once* did he tell them he	b) becoming very dependent on lenders.
3 *Never before* have so many people	c) take out a loan if you know you can't afford the repayments.
4 *Under no circumstances* should we	d) asked for a loan for cosmetic surgery.
5 *On no account* should you	e) to arrange loans over the telephone.
6 *At no time* in the history of their company did they end up	f) extend their credit.

B **Cross out the two incorrect explanations.**

A special word order is used in the six sentences in exercise A in order to

a) express time relations   b) add emphasis   c) sound more informal

Editing

C **Read this short text about European tax havens.**

In most of the lines **1–15** there is **one extra word** which does not fit. Some lines, however, are correct.

If a line is correct, put a tick (✓) on the appropriate line.

If there is an extra word in the line, write that word in the space provided.

Banks and other financial institutions with offshore bases in low-tax territories have	1 ....✓........
begun writing to their clients for making them aware of a little-publicised European	2 ......*for*......
Union savings directive, expected to come into force in July.	3 ....
Under the directive, financial institutions and in EU member states will be required	4 ....
to hand over to the relevant tax authority an information about savings income	5 ....
received by EU individuals not resident in the country where the account is held.	6 ....
The information will be handed to the tax authority where the account of holder is	7 ....
resident even so that it can be compared with what has been declared on their	8 ....
domestic tax returns.	9 ....
Payments affected include interest on bonds, savings of certificates, term deposits,	10 ....
current accounts and savings accounts. Other types of income, including company	11 ....
dividends, pensions and rents are not considered to be the savings income.	12 ....
The Inland Revenue says the directive – which may only applies to individuals and	13 ....
not companies and most trusts – will have any little impact on those who	14 ....
legitimately declare their savings income received outside the UK.	15 ....

FT Publishing
FINANCIAL TIMES

Requesting payment

D Complete each space in this fax requesting payment of an overdue invoice with the correct form of a verb from the box.

| arrange | assume | have | make | ~~regret~~ | remind |

Adria Wines
10 Trg Nikole Tesle
81 000 Podgorica
Montenegro

FACSIMILE NUMBER: ++381 81 642 254

Message for: Ghislain Debacker, Vins & Liqueurs
Address: 147 rue d'Assaut - 1040 Brussels - Belgium
Fax number: +322 689 98675
From: Zoran Lekic, Adria Wines
Date: 30 November
Number of pages including this page: TWO

Dear Mr Debacker,
We ..... _regret_ .....[1] to have to ....[2] you that payment of the following invoice is now 30 days overdue.

As we .... never ....[3] occasion to send you a reminder before, we ....[4] that this is just an oversight on your part.

Could you please ....[5] for payment to be ....[6] within a week.

Yours sincerely,

Z. Lekic,
Credit Controller

PAGE 1 OF 2

Invoice no. GDB\00\06
Customer no. GDB-75
Date 1 October

Item:	No:	Units:	Price per unit:	Total:
Vranac Quality Red Wine	PG-34A	200	€4	€800
Krstac Superior White Wine	PG-K55	100	€3.5	€350
			Grand Total:	€1,150

PAGE 2 OF 2

E Use the following notes to write Mr Debacker's reply to Mr Lekic.

- acknowledge receipt of fax
- order incomplete (only the white has arrived)
- waiting for rest of delivery
- full payment as soon as all goods are received
- prompt delivery essential as end of the year is approaching

Customer service

VOCABULARY **A** Choose the best word (*a, b, c* or *d*) to complete each space in the article.

CUSTOMER SERVICE

The way a company approaches customer service is one of the most important factors in determining its future success or failure.

No matter what a company does, it is always in the business of …*providing*…[1] customer service. If you take a look at companies that are not doing well or have gone …………………[2], one of their common features is their inability to deliver reliable and efficient customer service. All successful companies, on the other hand, understand and deliver what their customers want and strongly believe in the value of customer service training for management and …………………[3] employees.

Companies which fail to view customer service training as an …………………[4] are likely to remain in business only if they manage to keep a large number of first-time consumers. Moreover, they will probably end up losing market …………………[5] and experiencing a …………………[6] in profits unless they keep introducing new products and spending massively …………………[7] advertising.

Successful companies, however, are the ones which have grasped that in today's extremely competitive marketplace, being good is just not good enough anymore. Customers have become much more …………………[8] and expect nothing less than …………………[9] in customer service.

One of the keys to success is for a company to develop efficient means of communication between management and employees. This invariably has a direct positive effect on the customer. As a matter of fact, a company which is good to work for is usually one which is good to…………………[10] business with.

1	**a)** (providing)	**b)** giving	**c)** selling	**d)** caring
2	**a)** away	**b)** over	**c)** under	**d)** across
3	**a)** shopfloor	**b)** foreground	**c)** front-line	**d)** workshop
4	**a)** earning	**b)** expenditure	**c)** interest	**d)** investment
5	**a)** share	**b)** demand	**c)** niche	**d)** place
6	**a)** rise	**b)** drop	**c)** level	**d)** plateau
7	**a)** in	**b)** for	**c)** over	**d)** on
8	**a)** awkward	**b)** requested	**c)** complex	**d)** demanding
9	**a)** excellence	**b)** goodness	**c)** quality	**d)** expertise
10	**a)** deal	**b)** do	**c)** make	**d)** work

B Replace the parts in *italics* with the correct form of an idiomatic expression from the box.

> to slip somebody's mind   (to be) the last straw   to get to the bottom of the problem
> to get straight to the point   to pass the buck   to rip somebody off
> to go the extra mile   to talk at cross purposes

1 I intended to tell the manager a lot of customers had complained, but she was in a hurry and *I completely forgot*. …………*it slipped my mind*…………

2 If you are dissatisfied with their service, don't hesitate, *talk about it directly* and tell them what sort of compensation you expect.

……………………………………………………………

3 When we are sure we are to blame for a problem, our policy is never to *avoid responsibility*. ....

4 Avoid the Regency Hotel. They have a reputation for *charging far too much*.
   ....

5 It is not enough just to compensate customers when their complaints are justified. We have to *find the real cause of the problem* to make sure it doesn't happen again.
   ....

6 Not only did they refuse to admit that the video I had bought wasn't working properly, but they also refused to give me a replacement. That was *the last in a series of unpleasant events*! ....

7 I wanted a refund and they kept offering me a replacement. We were obviously *misunderstanding each other*. ....

8 Pilots have reacted in the right way by once again *making a special extra effort* to solve problems and extend their working duties to maximum legal limits in order to minimise the suffering of customers. ....

LANGUAGE REVIEW
Gerunds

A **Complete the sentences with a gerund from the box.**

working   taking   letting   being   ignoring   ~~listening~~

1 After ...*listening*... to the customer's complaint, we try to suggest a number of solutions.

2 She had mentioned .... as a customer care supervisor before.

3 They brazenly admitted .... all complaints.

4 We make a point of not .... the customer off the line until the query is fully resolved.

5 We know that .... patient and polite always makes a good impression.

6 Increasing production may mean .... on extra staff at the weekend.

B **Complete each sentence so that it means the same as the sentence just before it. Use a gerund each time.**

1 You won't go very far if you don't deal with your customers' complaints.
   You won't go very far without *dealing with your customers' complaints*

2 We spend a lot of money on training, and that's perfectly alright.
   We don't mind ....

3 One thing they complained about all the time was our prices.
   They never ceased ....

4 They said they didn't overcharge us.
   They denied ....

5 I don't think it's a good idea to promise too much to the customer.
   I think we should avoid ....

6 I'm sorry I didn't take the customer feedback seriously enough.
   I regret ....

In which of the six sentences above could an infinitive be used instead of a gerund?

C   **Circle the correct form(s) of the verb in the text.**

NEWS DIGEST

At Deltelfone, staff are encouraged *put /* (to put) */ putting*[1] themselves in the customer's shoes and find a solution instead of *opt / to opt / opting*[2] for an easy way out.

As a cellphone service provider, Deltelfone endeavours *provide / to provide / providing*[3] its customers with the highest level of service.

Miguel Fernandez, customer services director of the company, says the first priority is *ensure / to ensure / ensuring*[4] that customers receive their bills on time and that the accounts are accurate. Most people prefer *structure / to structure / structuring*[5] their monthly bill payments, and if bills are late it can inconvenience them, Fernandez says.

Bill / To bill / Billing[6] on time requires *have / to have / having*[7] the appropriate technology in place. Deltelfone interacts with its customers through its franchised dealer network and through its own call centre.

WRITING
Editing

A   **Read this short text about demanding customers.**

In most of the lines **1–14** there is **one extra word** which does not fit. Some lines, however, are correct.

If a line is **correct**, put a tick (✓) in the space provided.

If there is an **extra word** in the line, write that word in the space.

Demanding customers are certainly not new. What is new is their increasing numbers.

It can be argued that, to a large extent, it is the explosion in the   1 ....✓........

number of people using the Internet which has been a primarily   2 ....*a*........

responsible for increased customer frustration. It seems that if the   3 ....

speed of the Internet, and the number of cell phones, websites, and   4 ....

so on and have increased customer expectations. And when their   5 ....

expectations are not met, customers become quite demanding.   6 ....

What do customers will expect? Customers expect e-mails to be   7 ....

answered in a matter of hours, not for days. Very often, they   8 ....

expect to be able to find the answers to their questions on a   9 ....

company websites. Moreover, they must also expect to be able to   10 ....

talk to a live customer service rep or when they want to, and   11 ....

generally would like their problems to be resolved as quickly.   12 ....

One thing it is certain: companies that want to survive in the future   13 ....

will have to address these issues quickly.   14 ....

Letters of complaint

B   **Unscramble the sentences and re-order them to make *two* different letters of complaint. Write the sentence numbers in the table.**

1   As a matter of fact, the above invoice was settled on 10 October, i.e., exactly five days after our order had been received.

2   As a result, I will have to consider changing my supplier unless you can guarantee that such errors will not happen again in the future.

3   As usual, we paid by bank transfer.

4   Every time, those errors have had an adverse effect on our production schedules.

5   Further to our telephone call this morning, I am writing to complain about a number of items which are either missing or faulty in the above order.

6   I am sorry to have to remind you that this is the third time we have had occasion to complain of such mistakes.

7   Please find enclosed a detailed list of both missing and faulty items.

8   We enclose a copy of a statement from our bank confirming that payment was indeed made.

9   I hope you will take the necessary action to resolve this matter speedily.

10 We would advise you to check your records carefully.

11 With reference to your reminder of 1 December, it seems to us that an error has been made.

TYPE OF LETTER						
Complaint about delivery:	5	7				
Reply to a reminder to pay:	11					

C   Complete this reply to the complaint about delivery in exercise B.

BEEBOP FOOTWEAR – Wholesale & Retail

The Golden Boot
23 Birchington Road
Chelmsford
Essex CM4 5FG

Koningsstraat 53
1020 Brussels

23 May

Dear Mr Hopkins,

We were very sorry to receive your letter complaining ......_about_......¹ a damaged and incomplete consignment, order ref. 20G/FF/103.

Our staff have been ....² great pressure recently to deal with an unusually large number of orders, and unfortunately mistakes have occurred. We have already arranged ....³ all replacements and missing items to be shipped to you.

You will also be pleased to hear that, under the circumstances, we have decided to offer you a 6% discount instead of the 4% formerly agreed.

Please accept our apologies ....⁴ the inconvenience caused, and rest assured that we will do our utmost to ensure that such mistakes do not occur again ....⁵ the future.

We look forward ....⁶ doing business ....⁷ you again.

Yours sincerely,

Frans Vierstraete

Frans Vierstraete,
Sales Director

D   Write a reply to the second letter in exercise B.

Use a similar structure as in the letter above: apologise for the mistake, explain how it happened, explain what you have done or intend to do to put the mistake right, apologise again and end on a positive note.

Crisis management

VOCABULARY **A** **Use the clues to complete the crossword puzzle.**

Across

1 '.....................first!' is our motto. We've always believed that prevention is better than cure. (6)

2 'Take.....................! Those steps are slippery.' (4)

3 We need to work out an.....................plan to ensure the crisis does not happen again. (6)

4 When you deal with a crisis, you need to.....................responsibility where necessary and appropriate. (4)

5 Minimising the negative effects of a crisis is known as.....................limitation. (6)

7 Following the disaster, the company suffered a.....................of confidence in its products. (4)

9 We immediately issued a press.....................to inform the public. (7)

10 During the crisis, we kept our customers up to date with a regular.....................of information. (4)

Down

1 How quickly a company reacts to a crisis is known as its.................of response. (5)

2 A.....................plan is a backup strategy. (11)

3 An.....................of liability is an acceptance of responsibility in a crisis. (9)

6 As soon as the crisis arose, the manager spoke to the media at a.....................conference. (5)

8 The risk of being taken to court is the threat of.....................action. (5)

B Complete the noun phrases with a word from box A if the first part is missing, and with a word from box B if the second part is missing.

A	
decision	interest
~~effects~~	percentage
fear	range
	stress

B	
action	leader
crisis	managers
expertise	~~procedures~~

1 Airport and airline Safety Managers are usually aware of the advantages of having well prepared *emergency* ...*procedures*...[1] to minimise both the social and financial ...*effects*...[2] *of an accident* should one ever occur.

2 One wrong decision, even a small one, of a *business* ....[3] could be the cause of a serious *business* ....[4]. It is therefore not surprising that the ....[5] *of making mistakes* is one of the most important ....[6] *factors* for executives.

3 It is in the ....[7] *of every company* to deal with stress as effectively as possible. In companies where stress is ignored, there tends to be a relatively high ....[8] *of employees* being 'off sick'.

4 In a crisis management team, each member must be a ....[9] *maker* in their *area of* ....[10]. They must also be able to cope with conflicting information, make meaningful recommendations, and develop appropriate *courses of* ....[11].

5 According to a recent survey, *the majority of* ....[12] are not suitably prepared to respond to a wide ....[13] *of problems*.

LANGUAGE REVIEW
Conditionals

A Rewrite the following as conditional sentences.

1 Our fire alarms are serviced regularly, so we don't have problems with the Safety Department.

If our fire alarms... *weren't serviced regularly, we would have problems with the Safety Department*...

2 They recalled the faulty cars immediately, so no serious accidents happened.

If they ....

3 They never listened to their customers' comments and suggestions, so they weren't able to improve their services.

If they ....

4 We have an excellent safety record because we have got rid of all our older machines.

If we ....

5 We invested so much in safety equipment that the number of shopfloor injuries dropped by half.

If we ....

6 They didn't have a contingency plan, so they were unable to act.

If they ....

B Complete these sentences with the most appropriate word or phrase from the box.

| however much | no matter | otherwise | unless | whatever | ~~whether or not~~ |

1 ...*Whether or not*... you personally believe a constant flow of information is important, that's what both your customers and shareholders expect.

2 .... how hard we try, I fear the public won't regain confidence in our products.

3 We need to work out an action plan, ... we'll be in trouble if a crisis arises.

4 They will get in trouble with the Safety Department .... they service their fire alarms.

5 .... the future holds, let's continue to invest in safety training.

6 Of course we are in favour of safety training. But you should know that .... you invest in safety training, accidents will happen.

WRITING
Linking ideas

A Complete the text with the appropriate linkers from the box.

| secondly | ~~nevertheless~~ | as a result | finally | even | firstly | even | thirdly | yet |

Much has been written about safety at work. ...*Nevertheless*...¹, it still often remains an area of employment where the attitude taken is that 'accidents happen to others'. ....² there are many good reasons to suggest that much more attention should be paid to health and safety issues.

........................³, far too many employees are killed or injured each year as a direct result of their work.

........................⁴, managers can be prosecuted, fined, or ....⁵ jailed if it is found that they do not provide adequate safety standards.

........................⁶, any employee who suffers injury or ill health caused by or at work can make claims against the employer for negligence. ....⁷, additional costs may be incurred because of sick pay, lost production, etc.

........................⁸, companies with poor safety records soon have their reputation damaged with customers, shareholders, and ....⁹ the local community.

B Read the text below about handling a crisis.

In each line **1 – 11** there is **one wrong word**.

For each line, **underline the wrong word** in the text and write the **correct word** in the space provided.

The best thing you can do when you have a crisis on your hands
is to remain as responsive as possible and cooperate fully with
the authorities. If you are not complete sure what you are   1 *completely*
talking about, resisting the temptation to give out information   2 ....
just for the sake of seeming cooperatively. Make sure you have   3 ....
facts to deliver, and not just a vacuum to feel.   4 ....
Always remember to focus on the people affect by the crisis. If   5 ....
there are victims, theirs families will need to be informed,   6 ....
comforted and looked after. Money might needed to be made   7 ....
available to solve urgent issue.   8 ....
If you do not deal adequately over the provision of information or   9 ....
the people affected by the crisis, your company reputation might   10 ....
have seriously or even fatally damaged.   11 ....

C　Put the sentences in the body of the letter in the correct order.

Paul Gower's Advertising Agency

23 Alexandra Road
Bournemouth BH4 7NB

20 September

ATMOS Air-Conditioning Equipment
12 Yarmouth Gardens
Stevenage SG2 5LK

Dear Sirs,

[ ] Although the surveyors have not produced their final report yet, they seemed positive that the fire was caused by a faulty component rather than by careless installation.

[ ] In our interest as well as in yours, we recommend that you have all indoor units in that series thoroughly inspected, starting with ours.

[ ] The fire spread quickly, causing extensive damage to one of our offices.

[ ] We are writing in connection with the Delux Cool & Heat-4000 air-conditioning system we purchased on 5 September and which was installed by one of your engineers two days later.

[1] We look forward to hearing from you.

[ ] We would also be grateful if you could supply a replacement unit as soon a possible.

[ ] Yesterday evening, one of the indoor units caught fire.

Yours faithfully,

Fred Edgerton

Fred Edgerton

D　Use the following notes to write the reply from ATMOS to the advertising agency.

- express sympathy
- many Delux Cool & Heat-4000 sold and installed over the past three years / never a single complaint
- suggest operating instructions were not followed
- promise to deliver a replacement and send an engineer
- end on a positive note

Mergers & acquisitions

VOCABULARY **A** **Complete the newspaper extracts with the verbs from the box.**

taken   sold   set up   rejected   launched   approved

1   Astellas, the Japanese pharmaceuticals company, on Monday ....
a hostile bid for OSI Pharmaceuticals of the US, offering $3.5bn in a deal
designed to expand its US presence and activities in oncology.

2   Banks such as HSBC and Ta Chong Bank, which private equity firm Carlyle has
.... a stake in, are both planning to expand their branch networks in
Taiwan.

3   In February, Shell .... a $12bn joint venture with Cosan of Brazil to
produce and distribute ethanol and sugar.

4   In September 2009, the China Securities Regulatory Commission
.... the merger of the three groups, a move that created the
country's second-largest steelmaker.

5   Macarthur Coal, the Australian group, last week .... US Peabody
Energy's initial A$3.3bn bid as inadequate, saying it would go ahead with a
number of deals it struck last December with another group.

6   The owners of Gatwick have .... another stake in the airport,
this time to the Abu Dhabi Investment Authority, one of the world's leading
sovereign wealth funds.

VOCABULARY + **B** **Complete each space in the article with the best word (*a, b, c* or *d*).**

STRATEGIC ALLIANCES

As companies try to extend their reach, share risks or reduce costs, many of them decide
to form strategic alliances. Considering that such alliances often fail, one may wonder
whether this is due in part to a poor understanding of the management ...*skills*...[1]
required to make them work.

According to a recent report, alliance managers have to be impartial. They must not
be fiercely ....[2] to one company or ....[3] . They must be able
to tolerate different ways of doing things, and they also need to be willing to take
....................[4] and let things happen.

The report points out that the challenges ....[5] by alliances are different
from mergers because they are temporary, involve ....[6] ownership and
have fewer formal structures and little hierarchy.

Furthermore, many alliances are between past or present competitors, so it is crucial
to build ....[7]. Accessibility, face-to-face contact and personal example are
needed, and there is no place for ....[8] agendas.

It is also vital to know how to develop a ....[9] of employees, both
specialists and managers, who are capable of working in various complex yet temporary
alignments. This, according to the report, will become a key source of competitive
....................[10].

1	**a)** expert	**b)** (skills)	**c)** science	**d)** capability
2	**a)** committed	**b)** determined	**c)** indebted	**d)** destined
3	**a)** mark	**b)** name	**c)** make	**d)** brand
4	**a)** risks	**b)** stakes	**c)** shares	**d)** levels
5	**a)** resulted	**b)** posed	**c)** made	**d)** caused
6	**a)** divided	**b)** joined	**c)** shared	**d)** split
7	**a)** profit	**b)** energy	**c)** trust	**d)** venture
8	**a)** concealed	**b)** invisible	**c)** disguised	**d)** hidden
9	**a)** cadre	**b)** batch	**c)** frame	**d)** party
10	**a)** gain	**b)** force	**c)** advantage	**d)** value

LANGUAGE REVIEW

Prediction and probability

A Put the following predictions on a cline, from the least to the most certain to happen.

1 GBG Holdings *definitely won't* set up a joint venture with SVC Bank.

2 If the situation further deteriorates, there *might* be a market crash.

3 Pegasus Airways *isn't likely to* sell its stake in Basead.

4 Their recent acquisition *is bound to* lift share prices.

5 I think the new CEO *will probably* clash with the directors over business strategy.

100% sure **won't happen**	*1* ←————————————————————→	**100% sure** **will happen**

B Complete the second sentence in each pair so that it means about the same as the first sentence. Use between three and five words, including the word given.

1 There's a good chance that Karsten will benefit from the merger with SOC.
   probably
   Karsten .... from the merger with SOC.

2 The merger will not take place.
   chance
   There's .... taking place.

3 Their quarterly results will worry shareholders.
   bound
   Their quarterly results .... shareholders.

4 I'm sure the number of acquisitions won't increase significantly.
   definitely
   The number of acquisitions .... significantly.

5 Soribel will most probably become the dominant partner in the merger.
   certain
   Soribel .... the dominant partner in the merger.

6 I don't think Komerzialna Banka will make a bid.
   doubt
   .... Komerzialna Banka will make a bid.

7 Barclays said it most probably wouldn't bid for an investment bank.
   unlikely
   Barclays said it was highly .... for an investment bank.

WRITING
Editing

A **Read this short text about mergers.**

In most of the lines **1–14** there is **one extra word** which does not fit. Some lines, however, are correct.

If a line is **correct**, put a tick (✓) on the appropriate line.

If there is an **extra word** in the line, write that word in the space provided.

Why do so many mergers fail? Many consultants refer to how little time	1 ....✓.........
companies spend before a merger in thinking about whether their	2 ....in.........
organisations are compatible. The benefits of mergers are usually couched	3 ....
down in financial terms: cost-savings can be made or the two sides have	4 ....
complementary businesses that will allow them to increase up revenues.	5 ....
Mergers are about compatibility, which it means agreeing whose values	6 ....
will prevail and who will be the dominant partner. So it is no an accident	7 ....
that managers as well as journalists reach for a marriage metaphors in	8 ....
describing them. Merging their companies are said to 'tie the knot'.	9 ....
When mergers are called off, the two companies fail to 'make it up the	10 ....
aisle' or their relationship remains very 'unconsummated'. Yet the	11 ....
metaphor fails to convey over the scale of risk companies run when they	12 ....
launch acquisitions or mergers. Even in countries with the high divorce	13 ....
rates, marriages have a better success and rate than mergers.	14 ....

B **This announcement provides useful information for the writing task in exercise C. As you read it, complete it with the following prepositions.**

at (x 3)   from (x 2)   in

ALFITEL

The Third International Conference to be organised by ALFITEL Italy
will take place ...*from*...[1] 1 October to 3 October ....[2] :
ALFITEL Central Office

Via dei Colombi, 57

09135 – Cagliari

The conference is titled *The Future of Mergers & Acquisitions*.

The keynote speaker will be Odoardo Rizzotti, associate professor of
management studies ....[3] the Cagliari Business School
and dean of the MBA programme.

Speakers ....[4] other EU countries would be particularly
welcome. All presentations will be ....[5] English.

If you would like to give a presentation, please contact Paola Carboni,
conference organiser, ...[6] the above address or at:

Paola.Carboni@tin.it or phone / fax ++39 70 478 109.

C Marcel Lacour, a leading Belgian management consultant who took part in previous ALFITEL conferences, has phoned the conference organiser and discussed his presentation proposal. Here is the e-mail the organiser wrote to confirm the details. As you read it, complete it with the following future forms.

a) are going to allocate

b) are going to put

c) will be

d) will focus

e) will probably draw

From:
To:
Subject:

Dear Mr Lacour,

I would like to confirm what we discussed earlier this morning. Following your successful presentations at previous ALFITEL conferences, we have pleasure in inviting you to our third conference here in Cagliari in October.

The central theme ....[1] *'The Future of Mergers & Acquisitions'*, and your talk ....[2] essentially on the benefits of developing an in-house acquisition methodology.

As you ....[3] a sizeable audience as in previous years, we have made some special arrangements.

We ....[4] you in our main conference hall, which can seat at least 40 participants, and we ....[5] you a 45-minute slot (inclusive of 15 minutes' questions and answers).

We would be very grateful if you could confirm your acceptance in writing, and we of course remain at your disposal to discuss further details.

Yours sincerely,

Paola Carboni

Talk business

INTRODUCTION

The aim of this *Talk business* section is to make you more aware of some of the main features of English pronunciation. This will help you understand spoken English more easily. Hopefully, it will also help you discover areas you may need to work on for your spoken English to sound more natural.

THE SOUNDS OF ENGLISH

◀)) 1 **Look, listen and repeat.**

Vowel sounds

/ɪ/ quick fix
/iː/ clean sheet
/e/ sell well
/æ/ bad bank
/ɑː/ smart card
/ɒ/ top job
/ɔː/ short course
/ʊ/ good books
/uː/ school rules
/ʌ/ much luck
/ɜː/ first term
/ə/ aˈbout ˈCanada

Diphthongs

/eɪ/ play safe
/aɪ/ my price
/ɔɪ/ choice oil
/aʊ/ downtown
/əʊ/ go slow
/ɪə/ near here
/eə/ fair share

Consonants

1 Contrasting voiceless and voiced consonants

Voiceless		Voiced	
/p/	pay	/b/	buy
/f/	file	/v/	value
/t/	tax	/d/	deal
/θ/	think	/ð/	this
/tʃ/	cheap	/dʒ/	job
/s/	sell	/z/	zero
/k/	card	/g/	gain
/ʃ/	option	/ʒ/	decision

2 Other consonants

/m/ mine	/n/ net	/ŋ/ branding	/h/ high
/l/ loss	/r/ rise	/w/ win	/j/ year

Tips
- Identify the sounds that you have difficulty recognising or producing and focus mainly on these.
- Add your own key words in the tables above for the sounds you wish to focus on.
- Using the pause button on your CD player will give you time to speak or write when you do the exercises.

TALK BUSINESS

52

USING A DICTIONARY

Any good dictionary today gives you useful information on the pronunciation of individual words. With the help of the *Longman Business English Dictionary*, for example, you will be able to work out the pronunciation of any English word on your own once you are familiar with the phonetic symbols above.

In addition, the dictionary also gives you essential information about *word stress*. When a word has more than one syllable, we always put more stress on one of the syllables, i.e., we speak that syllable more strongly. Look at the dictionary entry for *compete*:

com·pete /kəmˈpiːt/ *v* [I] to try to win something or to be more successful than someone else:

- The sign ˈ shows you that the syllable immediately after it should be stressed: comˈPETE. You will find various exercises on word stress in Units 5, 6 and 12.

- The sign : shows you that the vowel is long. The contrast between *long* and *short* vowels is very important for mutual understanding. In Unit 1, for example, you will find an exercise on /ɪ/ and /iː/.

SOUNDS AND SPELLING

In English,
a) the same sound can be spelt in different ways, or
b) the same letters can be pronounced in different ways.
a) Consider for example /əʊ/, the sound of *go slow*. It can be spelt *o* as in *open*, *oa* as in *loan*, *oe* as in *toe*, *ough* as in *although*, *ow* as in *know*, or *eou* as in *Seoul*.
b) Take the letter *u* for instance. It can be pronounced /ʌ/ as in *cut*, /ʊ/ as in *full*, /ɜː/ as in *turn*, /ɔː/ as in *sure*, /juː/ as in *tune*, or /ɪ/ as in *busy*.

Put the following words under the correct sound in the table below (the letters in bold show the sound).

break	conscious	heart	knowledge	proceed	their
buyer	Europe	height	laugh	said	train
chair	friendship	insurance	million	scientific	want

Vowels		
/ɒ/	/e/	/ɑː/
1 job	1 sell	1 card
2	2	2 ....
3	3	3 ....
/eɪ/	/eə/	/aɪ/
1 pay	1 share	1 price
2	2	2 ....
3	3	3 ....

Consonants		
/ʃ/	/s/	/j/
1 option	1 sell	1 year
2	2	2 ....
3	3	3 ....

Sound–spelling relationships are explored in units 2, 3, 4, 5, 7, 9 and 12.

SHADOWING

Shadowing is a very effective way to make the most of the recorded material.
1 Play a short section, i.e. a few words or one line of a dialogue, then pause.
2 Without speaking, repeat internally what you heard.
3 Play the same section again. Pause and speak the words in exactly the same way and at the same speed. Repeat this step until you are completely satisfied with your performance.
4 Play the same section again and speak along with the voice on the recording. This is shadowing.
5 Move on to the next short section of the recording and repeat the same procedure.

TALK BUSINESS

Communication

SOUND WORK

A ◀)) 2 **Listen to the difference between /ɪ/ and /iː/.**

/ɪ/	/iː/
quick fix	clean sheet
big hit	weak team

B ◀)) 3 **Put the words you hear in the correct column.**

	/ɪ/	/iː/
1		
2		
3		
4		
5		
6		
7		
8		

◀)) 3 **Now listen again and practise saying the words.**

C ◀)) 4 **How many words can you hear in each of these sentences?**
Contractions (such as *he'll*, *isn't*, etc.) count as two words.

1 ....   3 ....

2 ....   4 ....

Tip

To practise saying a sentence faster, start from the end, like this:
- over lunch
- discuss it over lunch
- We'll discuss it over lunch.

◀)) 4 **Practise saying each sentence like this, using the audio script. Then listen to the recording again.**

D ◀)) 5 **Listen to how the voice goes up or down at the end of a question.**

1	↗
2	↘
3	↗
4	↘

E **Complete the rules.**

a) A *yes/no* question is usually asked with the voice going .... at the end;

b) A question starting with a question word is usually asked with the voice going .... at the end.

◀)) 5 **Listen again and practise saying the questions.**

TELEPHONING

A **Where do the following phrases fit in the telephone conversation below?**

1 Can I just read that back to you
2 Could you ask her to call me back later today
3 I'm afraid she isn't in her office
4 Sorry, it's not a very good line

5 How can I help you
6 I'd like to speak to
7 Just one moment, please
8 Not at all

Secretary: Good morning. Roma Kitchens. ......*5*......?

Caller: Hello. .... Paula Vecchi, please.

Secretary: Who shall I say is calling?

Caller: Hornby, Ron Hornby of Furniture World.

Secretary: .... Could you say that again, please?

Caller: Sure. Ron Hornby, of Furniture World.

Secretary: .... , Mr Hornby, I'll just find out if she's back yet ....
.... Is there anything I can do for you?

Caller: Well, it's rather urgent. The reason I'm calling is to fix a meeting at the Trade Fair next week. .... ? I'll be in the office till 5.30.

Secretary: And I'll take your phone number just in case ...

Caller: Sure. That's 020 8543 3553.

Secretary: .... ? 020 8543 3553.

Caller: That's correct. Thank you for your help.

Secretary: .... , Mr Hornby. I'll make sure she gets the message as soon as she's back. Goodbye.

Caller: Goodbye.

🔊 6 **Listen and check your answers.**

B **Write the message the secretary addressed to her boss.**

ROMA KITCHENS

To: ....

.... called. Company: ....

Day: ...*Tues*... Time: ...*10.45*...

S/HE: will call back ☐

wants you to phone back on: ....

left this message: ....

Standard ☐   Urgent ☐

C **Match the sentences on the left with a suitable reply on the right.**

1 I can't get through.
2 It seems we've got a crossed line.
3 The line's very faint.
4 Sorry, I didn't understand that.
5 I'm afraid his line's engaged.

a) Yeah. I'll hang up and call you back.
b) Right. I'll try and speak up a bit.
c) No problem. I'll hold.
d) Why's that? Still engaged?
e) Well, I'll go over it again, then.

International marketing

SOUND WORK

INDIVIDUAL SOUNDS

A 🔊 7 Listen how the letter *o* is pronounced in the following words.

pr**o**duct   m**o**netary   cl**o**thing   exp**o**rter   d**o**mestic   impr**o**ving

B Put the words from the box in the correct column, according to the pronunciation of the letter(s) in bold.

brainst**o**rm   devel**o**ping   g**o**vernment   inc**o**me   m**o**ve   **o**ffer   **o**verseas   p**o**litical   pr**o**fit   rep**o**rt   t**oo**   wh**o**lesaler

/ɒ/	/ʌ/	/əʊ/	/ɔː/	/ə/	/uː/
product	monetary	clothing	exporter	domestic	improving

🔊 8 Listen and check your answers. Then listen again and practise saying the words.

CONNECTED SPEECH

C 🔊 9 Listen to the recording and complete the noun phrases.

1 This year's been marked by expanding .... operations.

2 We've had to cope with an extremely .... exchange rate.

3 All I can say is that it's been an .... successful trade fair.

4 Do you know who's the head of their new public .... department?

5 We're going to launch a highly .... market research programme.

STRESS AND INTONATION

D 🔊 10 Listen to the stress in these noun compounds and phrases.

* a **grow**ing **mar**ket
* a **trade** fair
* a **free sam**ple
* a **fo**cus group

What's the rule?

If the noun compound or phrase consists of Adjective + Noun, we *often* stress both the adjective and the noun.

If it consists of Noun + Noun, we *often* stress only the first noun.

E <u>Underline</u> the stressed syllable(s) in the following compounds and phrases.

1 an ex<u>pan</u>ding <u>mar</u>ket

2 a sales network

3 a special offer

4 a single market

5 a balance sheet

6 the exchange rate

🔊 11 Listen and check your answers. Then listen again and practise the compounds and phrases.

BRAINSTORMING

A **Read the interview about *brainstorming* with Pat Whitney, Marketing Consultant. As you read, match Pat's replies to the interviewer's questions.**

Interviewer: So, Pat, what exactly is brainstorming, then?

Pat: ....6.............

Interviewer: Do they prepare in advance?

Pat: ....

Interviewer: So it's okay to come up with crazy ideas?

Pat: ....

Interviewer: I suppose there's someone to lead the session, though.

Pat: ....

Interviewer: Mm. That sounds interesting. Does that mean there are no guidelines to go by?

Pat: ....

Interviewer: Such as?

Pat: ....

Interviewer: But surely the ideas need to be evaluated?

Pat: ....

Interviewer: Just one more question, then. Is there any interaction at all between the group members?

Pat: ....

Interviewer: A kind of 'cross-fertilisation' I suppose. Well, thanks very much for your time, Pat.

1 Absolutely! In fact, the wilder they are, the better.

2 Not quite. In fact, there are rules to follow if the brainstorming is to be successful.

3 Of course, but that's done in a follow-up meeting.

4 Preparation often isn't necessary. The thing is, at the brainstorming stage it's not the quality of the ideas that matters, but the quantity.

5 Well, for instance, only one person at a time is allowed to speak, and everyone has an equal chance to speak.

6 Well, it's very simple. A smallish group of people, sometimes from a variety of backgrounds, get together and spontaneously express their thoughts about ways of solving a specific problem.

7 Yeah. There's a group leader to state the problem clearly at the beginning, and restate it later if necessary, but other than that everyone has equal status in the group.

8 Yes, there is. Quite a lot, in fact. Participants are constantly encouraged to suggest combinations or modifications of ideas put forward by other members.

B ◀》 12 **Listen and check your answers. Then listen again, and spot five differences between the recording and the script in exercise A.**

C ◀》 13 **Listen to 10 extracts from meetings and decide what the woman is doing in each one.**

* Write one letter (**a–e**) next to the number of the extract.
* Use each letter twice.

Extract 1 ....
Extract 2 ....
Extract 3 ....
Extract 4 ....
Extract 5 ....

Extract 6 ....
Extract 7 ....
Extract 8 ....
Extract 9 ....
Extract 10 ....

a) Stating objectives
b) Making a suggestion
c) Expressing enthusiasm
d) Encouraging contributions
e) Agreeing

SURVIVAL BUSINESS ENGLISH

Building relationships

INDIVIDUAL SOUNDS

A 🔊 14 Listen and write down the four words that you hear. Then check your spelling.

1 .... 3 ....

2 .... 4 ....

Have you noticed?

All four words have /ɪ/, the sound of *quick fix*, but each time with a different spelling.

B 🔊 15 Now listen and write down six more words which have the /ɪ/ sound.

1 .... 4 ....

2 .... 5 ....

3 .... 6 ....

🔊 15 Listen and check your spelling. Then listen again and practise saying the words.

CONNECTED SPEECH

C 🔊 16 Listen to how the words in *italics* are pronounced in these conversation excerpts.

1 How *do you* do?

2 Where *do you* come from?

3 *Did you* have a good trip?

4 What *do you* do in your spare time?

5 *Would you* like me to call a taxi?

> **Tips**
>
> In informal speech, *do you* is often pronounced /djə/ or /dʒə/. *Did/Could/Would you* are often pronounced /dɪdjə/ , /kʊdjə/ , /wʊdjə/ or /dɪdʒə/ , /kʊdʒə/ , /wʊdʒə/.
>
> You may choose not to use such weak forms and contractions yourself, but being aware of them will help you understand native speakers better.

🔊 16 Listen again and practise asking the questions.

D 🔊 17 Listen and complete these questions.

• ....Did........ you .... somewhere to stay?

• .... do you .... your hotel?

• .... you recommend a good restaurant?

• Where .... you spend your holidays?

• .... you like to join us for dinner tomorrow?

• .... you have his phone number, by any chance?

• What .... you talk about?

• .... would you like to come?

🔊 17 Check your answers. Then listen again and practise asking the questions.

FIRST TIME CONVERSATION

A 🔊 18 Listen to this conversation between two people who meet for the first time and think about what makes it successful or unsuccessful.

B 🔊 19 Listen and complete this conversation between two other people who meet for the first time.

A: Sarah, I hear you're from Australia?

B: .... [1], yeah. I live in Bendigo, northwest of Melbourne.

A: Melbourne! You must find our weather pretty dismal, then.

B: .... [2]. Actually, I didn't expect so much sunshine here. Have you ever been to Australia?

A: No, no, ... [3] someday. You see, I'm into alternative sources of energy, and I've heard a lot about Australian research into agricultural technology ...

B: ... That's a rapidly growing area, ... [4]?

A: Yes. It certainly is. .... [5]? Are you in the agrotech business as well?

B: No, not at all. I'm an accountant, but I was made redundant last year. So now my brother and I are working on a project together.

A: Mm, that .... [6]. What sort of project is that?

B: Well, he works as a consultant in the tourist industry, and we both love Australia. And one day we identified a gap in the market ...

C Complete this more successful version of the conversation in exercise A with the sentences from the box.

a)	A small world, some say. Were you there on a course?
b)	Accountancy. Sounds boring, doesn't it?
c)	Edmonton. That's in Alberta, in western Canada.
d)	Extremely. And we're all very committed to the company.
e)	I'm from Canada, actually.
f)	So I've heard. And how did you like Canada?
g)	The work is alright and the atmosphere is absolutely brilliant. We're a smallish company – there're only 30 of us.

A: So, Stanley, what about you? Where do you come from?

B: .... *e* ....

A: Really? Whereabouts in Canada?

B: ....

A: What a coincidence! I spent three months at the University of Calgary a couple of years ago ...

B: ....

A: That's right, yes. They do an excellent intensive management training course.

B: ....

A: I really had a great time in sunny Alberta! How about you, by the way? What line are you in?

B: ....

A: You certainly don't look bored! What's it like?

B: ....

A: Nice people?

B: ....

D 🔊 20 Listen and check your answers. Then listen again and take Speaker B's part.

Success

INDIVIDUAL SOUNDS

A The *-ed* ending has three pronunciations: /d/, /t/, /ɪd/. **In each line, cross out the word whose ending has a different pronunciation from the other three.**

1 interested	motivated	recognised	divided
2 appeared	believed	introduced	changed
3 wanted	worked	finished	assessed
4 renamed	underestimated	devalued	underperformed

◀)) **21 Check your answers in the key. Then listen and practise saying the words.**

B ◀)) **22 Listen to how these verb forms are pronounced.**

1 syllable	booked	launched	passed
2 syllables	travelled	produced	posted
3 syllables	decided	outperformed	undercharged

C How many syllables do the following verb forms have?

1 discussed	........2........		**5** misjudged	....
2 watched	....		**6** co-authored	....
3 researched	....		**7** staffed	....
4 respected	....		**8** mismanaged	....

◀)) **23 Check your answers in the key. Then listen and practise saying the words.**

STRESS AND INTONATION

D ◀)) **24 Listen to how Speaker B corrects information in the following excerpts from negotiations.**

A: OK. That's agreed, then. You'll get everything to us by the end of May.
B: Sorry, no. We said we could deliver by the end of <u>June</u>.

A: Right. So the price we agreed is for your deluxe model.
B: No, that's not quite right. £999 is for our <u>standard</u> model, actually.

The underlined words give the correct information. Speaker B therefore puts extra stress on them. In the following exchanges, <u>underline</u> the word which Speaker B will put extra stress on.

1 A: So you're willing to give us a 12% discount if we buy over 14 vehicles.
 B: That's not quite right, I'm afraid. We were talking about 40 vehicles.

2 A: Right. If we ask you to change the specifications, you'll reduce the discount by 2%.
 B: No, I'm afraid in that case we'd have to reduce it by 4%.

3 A: That's agreed, then. If we pay an extra £300, you'll give us a five-year warranty.
 B: Sorry, no. That'd be an extra £500, in fact.

4 A: So if we pay an extra £300, you'll give us a five-year warranty.
 B: I'm afraid we only give a two-year warranty for that amount.

5 A: Are you saying that if we increase our order to 500, you'll lower your price to £55 per item?
 B: Well, no. For orders of that size we could only decrease it to 75.

◀)) **25 Listen and check your answers.**

SAYING MORE THAN *YES* OR *NO*

A Look at these exchanges. What is wrong with Speaker B's replies?

1 A: Do you need a hand?

2 A: Excuse me, is Accounts on this floor?

3 A: Have you been here before?

4 A: Would you like me to type it for you?

5 A: It's a bit chilly in here, isn't it?

6 A: Could I browse through these files just for a minute?

B: Yes.

B 🔊 26 Listen and complete the sentences.

a) Oh, ...*thanks*.... very much. That's very .... of you.

b) That's ...., yes. Straight .... this corridor, last door on your left.

c) Yes, of .... Please go ....

d) Yes, it is, ... it. How .... closing that window?

e) I'd really .... that. Thank you very much.

f) Yes, I have, ... This is my third visit.

C Match each response from exercise B with the correct question from exercise A.

a) = 1   b) =   c) =   d) =   e) =   f) =

D Reply to the following questions in a positive and friendly way, like in the example.

1 A: Would you like me to double-check those figures?

   B: ....*Oh, thanks a lot. That's very kind of you.*....

2 A: Could I use the photocopier?

   B: ....

3 A: Is Arabic your first language, then?

   B: ....

4 A: It's a bit stuffy in here, don't you find?

   B: ....

5 A: Would you like us to order a taxi for you?

   B: ....

🔊 27 Listen to some possible ways of answering the questions in exercise D. Then listen again and practise Speaker B's answers.

E Look at these comments made during negotiations. What is wrong with them?

1 More credit? No way!

2 Give us a discount.

3 Delivery in one week? Pay on delivery, then.

4 Lower our prices more? Sounds like a bad joke.

5 8% discount? OK, but then order over 100. Alright?

6 We want you to alter the specifications.

🔊 28 Briefly think of more diplomatic ways of making these comments. Then listen and practise the sample answers.

SURVIVAL BUSINESS ENGLISH

UNIT 5 Job satisfaction

CONNECTED SPEECH

A 🔊 29 **Listen and complete these passive sentences.**

1 She _'s been_ praised for her creativity.

2 They .... asked to work overtime.

3 They .... trained to work under pressure.

4 Some of them .... forced to choose between work and home.

5 A decent balance between work and personal life .... rated very highly.

🔊 29 **Listen again and practise saying the sentences. Use the contractions in sentences 1–3, and the weak forms /wə/ and /wəz/ in sentences 4 and 5 respectively.**

B **Put the words in the box in the correct column according to their stress pattern.**

| appraisal   award   balance   benefits |
| career   colleague   promotion   salary |

0o	o0	0oo	o0o
bonus	success	flexible	fulfilment

🔊 30 **Listen and check your answers. Then listen again and practise saying the words.**

Tip

Words of two or more syllables can have different stress patterns. In *bonus*, for example, the first syllable is stressed (i.e., relatively long and strong), and the second syllable is unstressed (i.e., relatively short and weak); in *success*, it is the other way around. In the dictionary, stress is marked with the symbol /'/ just before the stressed syllable.

C 🔊 31 **Listen and complete the words.**

| bon_us_ | c_mmiss_ _n | _ssessm_nt | _llow_nce |
| c_reer | redund_ncy | p_ _form_nce | c_mplaint |

Tip

All the letters that you wrote in are pronounced /ə/. This sound is called *schwa*, and is the most common sound in English. It appears in unstressed syllables only, and can be written *a, e, i, o, u* etc.
Noticing and using /ə/ can help you improve your pronunciation and your comprehension.

COLD-CALLING **A** **Complete the telephone conversation with the verbs from the box.**

was given	find out know	meet	recommend
sound out	suggested	think	understand

RV: Rosalia Valdesi.

PW: Good morning, Ms Valdesi. My name's Paul Whitby. I work for an executive recruitment agency.

RV: Oh yes?

PW: I ....¹ your name by Luis Deltell. I believe you ....² him quite well.

RV: That's right. Yes. And what is it about?

PW: Mr Deltell ....³ I call you. He thought you might be interested in a position that's become vacant at GSP Consulting. It's for a senior financial adviser. Would you like to ....⁴ to ....⁵ a bit more about the post?

RV: Well, thank you very much for contacting me. But to be honest, I don't ....⁶ there's any point in us meeting. You see, I'm very happy in my current job, and I'm not thinking of going anywhere else.

PW: Sure, I quite ....⁷. Maybe then there's someone else you could ....⁸? Someone I could contact and ....⁹ about the job?

RV: Well, let me see ...

🔊 **32 Listen and check your answers. Then listen again and take Paul Whitby's part.**

B **In conversation, we often paraphrase information instead of just repeating it. Look at this example.**

A: All in all it sounds like a *rewarding* job.

B: Yes, I really find it very *satisfying*.

How could Speaker B respond to the following utterances? Use the words from the box.

perks	red tape	independence	~~opportunities for promotion~~	fire

1 A: What's the *career structure* like where you work?
   B: Well, there are *lots of opportunities for promotion, I must say.*

2 A: What *fringe benefits* do they offer?
   B: ....

3 A: I hear Peter's going to be *dismissed*.
   B: ....

4 A: Personally, I'd enjoy a little more *autonomy*.
   B: ....

5 A: It's so demotivating having to deal with *bureaucracy*, don't you find?
   B: ....

🔊 **33 Listen to the sample answers on the recording. Then listen again and take Speaker B's part.**

INDIVIDUAL SOUNDS

A 🔊 34 **Listen and add the missing consonants in the words below.**

1 _s p_ endid; _ _ _ing; _ _ _aight

2 _ _ _it; _ _ _ee; _ _ _ong

3 _ _y and _ _ _ead the ri_ _ _ .

4 She was _ _igh_ _y _ _itical of our re_ _uitment _ _ _ategy.

5 _ _ _angely enough, they in_ _oduced new _ _ade re_ _ _ i_ _ions.

6 Our company is _ _ _u_ _ _ing to survive. It is an e_ _ _emely _ _ _ e_ _ _ul situation.

🔊 34 **Listen again and practise the words and sentences. Pay attention in particular to the consonant groups.**

CONNECTED SPEECH

B 🔊 35 **Listen to how certain words are linked together in these expressions of agreement and disagreement.**

1 I quite‿agree.

2 I don't‿agree.

What's the rule?

When a word finishes with a **consonant** and the word immediately after begins with a **vowel** sound, we usually **link** those two words.

C 🔊 36 **Indicate where similar links could be made in these sentences.**

1 That's‿out‿of the question‿, I'm‿afraid.

2 Well, I couldn't agree more.

3 That's not at all how I see it.

4 I'm in complete agreement.

5 That's absolutely right.

6 Are we all agreed on this issue?

7 Alright then. Let's agree to disagree.

🔊 36 **Check your answers. Then listen again and practise saying the sentences.**

STRESS AND INTONATION

D **Circle the word which has a different stress pattern.**

	a)	**b)**	**c)**
1	quantify	calculate	encounter
2	develop	minimise	estimate
3	reduce	limit	control
4	terrible	minimal	tremendous
5	remote	serious	increased
6	measure	avoid	assess

🔊 37 **Listen and check your answers.**

AGREEING AND DISAGREEING

A ◀)) **38 Listen to five different conversations, and decide what the main topic of each one is.**

- Write one letter, **a)–i)**, next to the number of the conversation.
- Do not use any letter more than once.

Conversation **1** ....   a) computer monitors

Conversation **2** ....   b) eating out

Conversation **3** ....   c) employees' e-mails

Conversation **4** ....   d) how smokers are treated

Conversation **5** ....   e) looking after sick relatives

f) the cold weather

g) the social aspects of work

h) using the phone at work for personal calls

i) vegetarian food

B **You heard the following expressions of agreement or disagreement:**

a) Absolutely.

b) Do you think so?

c) I couldn't agree more.

d) I can't go along with that.

e) So would I.

f) That's right.

g) Well, actually, I'm not sure I agree with that.

h) You must be joking!

Put them on a scale starting with strong agreement and ending with strong disagreement like this:

c							h

ACCEPTING OR DECLINING INVITATIONS

C ◀)) 39 **Complete the prompts below. Then listen and check your answers, and match each of the invitations with the response you heard.**

1 .... we go for a drink?

2 .... you like to join us for lunch tomorrow?

3 I wondered .... you could come to our housewarming party on Saturday?

4 What .... coming round for a drink Friday after work?

5 We'd like to .... you to our house after the seminar.

6 Do you .... a bite to eat?

 a) That would be nice. Thanks.

b) Great idea.

c) I'd be delighted.

d) I'd love to, but I've got another engagement.

e) Sorry, I can't. No lunch break for me today!

f) I'm afraid I can't. I'm going away for the weekend.

UNIT 7 Management styles

A 🔊 40 Listen to the difference between /ʃ/, /ʒ/, /tʃ/, and /dʒ/.

/ʃ/ as in op**ti**on	/ʒ/ as in deci**si**on	/tʃ/ as in **ch**eap	/dʒ/ as in **j**oint
efficient	measure	cheque	jet
passion	vision	March	large

B Put the words in the box in the correct column according to the pronunciation of the letter(s) in bold.

~~**manager**~~	cat**ch**y	pre**ss**ure	lei**s**ure	ur**g**ent
ra**ti**onal	lo**g**ical	preci**si**on	so**ci**able	coa**ch**

/ʃ/	/ʒ/	/tʃ/	/dʒ/
			manager

🔊 41 Listen and check your answers. Then listen again and practise saying the words.

C 🔊 42 Listen to the way certain sounds are linked in this sentence.

Allan‿is‿extremely sociable‿and‿always joins‿us for lunch.

What's the rule?

See page 64.

D Now show where similar links could be made in these sentences.

1 Our office manager doesn't involve us in any decisions.

2 They encouraged us to plan everything with absolute precision.

3 Of course it's a high-pressure job, but there's a lot of prestige attached to it.

🔊 43 Listen and check your answers. Then listen again and practise saying the sentences.

E 🔊 44 Listen to the words in the following table. <u>Underline</u> the stressed syllable.

Adjective	Noun
charis<u>mat</u>ic	cha<u>ris</u>ma
competent	competence
diplomatic	diplomacy
flexible	flexibility
inspiring	inspiration
sociable	sociability

🔊 44 Listen again and practise saying the words.

PRESENTATIONS

A 🔊 **45 Listen to 10 extracts from presentations, and decide what the presenter is doing in each one.**

- Write one letter (**a–e**) next to the number of the extract.
- Use each letter twice.

Extract 1 ....   Extract 6 ....   **a)** Stating the purpose

Extract 2 ....   Extract 7 ....   **b)** Involving the audience

Extract 3 ....   Extract 8 ....   **c)** Changing to another topic

Extract 4 ....   Extract 9 ....   **d)** Emphasising

Extract 5 ....   Extract 10 ....   **e)** Discussing implications

> **Tip**
>
> As exercise A shows, effective presenters flag their presentation, i.e., they use specific signalling phrases to highlight the structure of their talk. For example, they use specific phrases to let the audience know the aim of the presentation, or to introduce another topic, or to move on to another topic, etc.

B **Put the following signalling phrases next to the correct heading in the box below.**

1 For instance, ...

2 I'd like to go back to a point I mentioned earlier.

3 If you look at the graph, you'll see ...

4 I'd like to wrap up now by running through the main points again.

5 If you look at the slide, you can see ...

6 Let me draw your attention to your handout.

7 As I said to begin with, ...

8 Let me give you an example...

9 So, to sum up ...

10 What this diagram shows is ...

11 As I said in my introduction, ...

12 This brings me to the end of my talk. Let me just recap briefly on the main points.

Exemplifying	*1*
Returning to a point made earlier	
Referring to visuals or handouts	
Concluding	

C 🔊 **46 Listen to a presentation about e-mail etiquette and tick the phrases in exercise B that the speaker uses.**

Team building

INDIVIDUAL SOUNDS

A **What are the words transcribed below?**

Use the chart in the Introduction to help you, or check in your dictionary.

1 /ˈsəʊʃəbəl/ *sociable*

2 /ɪˈmædʒ ˌə nətɪv/

3 /ˈlɔɪəl/

4 /ɪˈfɪʃənt/

5 /ˈpɒpjʊlə/

6 /ˈtɒlərənt/

> **Tip**
>
> Notice how often the schwa sound (/ə/) appears in unstressed syllables

🔊 **47 Listen and practise saying the words.**

CONNECTED SPEECH

B 🔊 **48 Listen to how *have* is pronounced in these sentences.**

1 We should‿have‿encouraged more debate and discussion. /əv/

2 The trainer shouldn't‿have spent so much time on 'difficult people'! /əv/

3 Her presence might‿have boosted the team's performance. /əv/

4 We needn't‿have hurried to the airport. The plane was late. /əv/

5 Where's my key? I must‿have dropped it somewhere. /əv/

6 The team would‿have been stronger without him. /əv/

> **What's the rule?**
>
> When *have* is used between a modal verb and a past participle, the weak form /əv/ is always used.

🔊 **49 Listen and practise saying other examples.**

STRESS AND INTONATION

C 🔊 **50 Listen to how Speaker B highlights the word which is most significant in the context.**

1 A: It's not a very imaginative solution.

   B: But it is <u>practical</u>.

2 A: It's not a very practical solution.

   B: But it <u>is</u> practical.

D **Underline the words Speaker B will highlight in these conversations.**

1 A: Is there anything you dislike in your job?

   B: I hate the paperwork.

2 A: How do you feel about all the admin stuff?

   B: I hate the paperwork.

3 A: Have you registered for the May seminar?

   B: I have signed up for the June one.

4 A: Why don't you register for the June seminar?

   B: I have signed up for the June one.

5 A: He wasn't a very enthusiastic team leader.

   B: But he was efficient.

6 A: Efficiency was certainly not Harry's forte.

   B: But he was efficient.

🔊 **51 Listen to check your answers. Then listen again and take B's role.**

DIPLOMATIC LANGUAGE

A ◀ᴗ **52 'Diplomatic language' is often used in conflict resolution. Listen and complete the examples on the right.**

1 It'll be very difficult to make him change his mind.

It ...*might be*... quite difficult to make him change his mind.

2 Can you tell me how you feel about it?

.... you tell me how you feel about it?

3 That solution will be too difficult to implement.

.... that solution be a bit difficult to implement?

4 Tell them what your goals are.

.... tell them what your goals are.

5 I want to know what you plan to do.

.... to know what you plan to do.

> **Tips**
>
> In certain situations, a more direct approach is needed (see sentences on the left); in other situations, such an approach might seem too direct or even aggressive, and 'diplomatic' language is more appropriate (see sentences on the right).

B **Make these sentences sound less 'direct'.**

1 Try and build on the strengths of the team.
2 Sending the team on a weekend training course will be far too expensive.
3 I want each employee to have a say.
4 What's your main concern?
5 Those changes will be perceived as too drastic.
6 It will be very risky to suggest removing any of the senior team members.

C ◀ᴗ **53 Listen and practise saying the model sentences.**

D **It is sometimes desirable to reject ideas and suggestions in a diplomatic way. See how Speaker B does that in these two examples.**

1 A: I think you should talk to each team member individually.
   B: *I'm afraid that's not really feasible.*

2 A: I'm sure that if you removed Tom and Amy, the team would be a lot more effective.
   B: *I appreciate your point of view, but I couldn't possibly do that.*

◀ᴗ **54 Listen to five different suggestions and decide what the best response to each one is.**

- Write one letter, **a)**–**e)**, next to the number of the speaker.
- Do not use any letter more than once.

Speaker 1 ....

Speaker 2 ....

Speaker 3 ....

Speaker 4 ....

Speaker 5 ....

a) I appreciate your point of view, but I couldn't possibly do that. Everyone would wonder who's going to be sent away next.

b) I can see why you would want to do this, but I don't think it would work. It would cause a lot of jealousy amongst the staff in other departments.

c) I see what you mean, but that's not really practical. Nothing would ever get done on time.

d) I'm afraid that's not really feasible. It would take me over a week!

e) That sounds very interesting, but I doubt we can afford it. How about a weekend event?

◀ᴗ **55 Listen to the dialogues and check your answers. Then listen again and practise the responses to the suggestions.**

SURVIVAL BUSINESS ENGLISH

UNIT 9 Raising finance

INDIVIDUAL SOUNDS

A 🔊 56 Listen to how the letter *a* is pronounced in the following words.

asset   priv**a**te   m**a**rket   st**a**ke   t**a**lk   mort**ga**ge

B Put the words below in the correct column, according to the pronunciation of the letter(s) in bold.

acquisition account purchase percentage encourage although
finance instalment overdraft rate grant angel

/æ/ as in bad bank	/ə/ as in about Canada	/ɑː/ as in smart card	/eɪ/ as in play safe	/ɔː/ as in short course	/ɪ/ as in quick fix
asset	private	market	stake	talk	mortgage

🔊 57 Now check your answers. Then listen again and practise the words.

CONNECTED SPEECH

C 🔊 58 Listen to the way certain sounds are linked in these sentences.

1 Everyone‿expects‿a return‿on their‿investment.

2 The report contained‿an‿assessment‿of the risks facing European‿investors.

> **What's the rule?**
> When a word finishes with a **consonant** and the word immediately after begins with a **vowel** sound, we usually **link** those two words.

D Indicate where similar links could be made in these sentences.

1 The first instalment is due in April.

2 The company has gone into administration with debts of about eight million euros.

3 If we are serious about this acquisition, we'll have to put our money where our mouth is.

🔊 59 Check your answers. Then listen again and practise saying the sentences.

STRESS AND INTONATION

E 🔊 60 Listen and put each question 1–8 in the correct column, depending on whether the voice goes up or down at the end.

↗	↘
1	....
....	....
....	....
....	....

🔊 60 Check your answers. Then listen again and practise saying the questions.

> **Tip**
> There is a tendency for the voice to go down at the end of *wh-* questions and up at the end of *yes/no* questions.

NEGOTIATING AN AGREEMENT

A ◀)) **61 In negotiations, too, it is often desirable to use 'diplomatic language' (see ◀)) 52). Listen and complete the sentences on the right.**

1 There's no way we can invest in your project in its present form.

Unfortunately, we couldn't invest in your project in its present form.

2 We must talk about start-up costs first.

.... talk about start-up costs first.

3 We want some additional collateral.

.... offer some additional collateral?

4 We won't lower our interest rate.

.... that's the lowest rate we can offer.

5 You must try to bring in another backer.

.... you could bring in another backer?

6 Your interest rate is far too high.

Your interest rate is higher ....

B ◀)) **62 Listen to 10 sentences, and decide which negotiating technique each one illustrates.**

Sentence 1	Sentence 6	**a)** Open questions
Sentence 2	Sentence 7	**b)** Closed questions
Sentence 3	Sentence 8	**c)** Softening phrases
Sentence 4	Sentence 9	**d)** Signalling phrases
Sentence 5	Sentence 10	**e)** Summarising

Listen again and complete sentences 1-5.

1 When will you be in a position to .... the .... ?

2 Let's .... over what we've .... so far, then.

3 Can I .... on that? I think we must look for other .... of finance.

4 Do you have a .... problem?

5 Can you repay the .... in four .... ?

TAKING ACTION

C ◀)) **63 In negotiations, you cannot always answer all questions immediately. Listen to how Speaker B expresses the need for a little thinking time, and complete the exchanges.**

1 A: Do you think you'll be able to break even in two years?

B: Well, maybe, erm, *that really depends on the market.*

2 A: So exactly how many backers will you be able to find?

B: Can I ....

3 A: Will you accept payment by instalments?

B: We'll ....

4 A: We'd like to know why the overdraft hasn't been repaid yet.

B: I'll ....

5 A: How much will you need for start-up costs?

B: Well, ...

6 A: So we're all agreed on the collateral, then?

B: ....

SURVIVAL BUSINESS ENGLISH

SOUND WORK

A 🔊 **64 Listen to how the consonants /p/, /t/ and /k/ are pronounced.**

policy	**t**ask	**c**ustomer
re**p**air	re**t**ain	re**c**all

Tip

In English, the voiceless consonants /p/, /t/, and /k/ are pronounced with a noticeable *aspiration* when they occur at the beginning of a word or of a stressed syllable.

🔊 **64 Listen again and practise saying the words.**

B 🔊 **65 Listen and complete the following examples.**

1 **c**ustomer **c**......................

2 **c**ompany **p**......................

3 **p**eak **t**....................

4 **c**.................... intentions

5 **c**.................... **p**rice

6 re**p**air **p**......................

7 **p**.................... re**p**ort

🔊 **65 Listen again and practise saying the phrases, paying particular attention to the aspirations.**

C 🔊 **66 Listen to the pronunciation of *do you / did you / would you*.**

1 How do you like working in a call centre?

2 Did you mention having worked abroad?

3 Would you mind filling in this form?

4 How do you deal with complaints?

5 Did you take part in any training?

🔊 **66 Listen again and practise saying the questions.**

Tip

In each example, the weak form /jə/ is used and is linked with the word before it:
/djə/ /dɪdjə/ /wʊdjə/.
Such sound simplifications often occur in informal speech. You may choose not to use them, but being aware of them may help improve your listening skills.

STRESS AND INTONATION

D 🔊 **67 Listen to Speakers A and B apologise and indicate who sounds genuinely concerned.**

1 I'm afraid you sent me the wrong model.
   A: ....✓............. B: ....

2 The books we ordered haven't reached us yet.
   A: .... B: ....

3 Some of the goods were badly damaged.
   A: .... B: ....

4 This delay has really messed up our sales.
   A: .... B: ....

5 We've again received a reminder for that invoice which was settled three months ago.
   A: .... B: ....

6 We still haven't received your invoice.
   A: .... B: ....

E 🔊 **68 Listen and practise each polite reply. Try to sound genuinely polite.**

DEALING WITH COMPLAINTS

A 🔊 **69 For each speaker that you hear, tick the most appropriate reply.**

1 a) What seems to be the problem? ✓
   b) What makes you think it's serious?
   c) I don't mind.

2 a) I hope so.
   b) What's the matter?
   c) If you would.

3 a) I'm sure it could have been worse.
   b) I'm sorry to hear you've been inconvenienced.
   c) I think there's a problem with your schedule.

4 a) I'm afraid so. I'm pretty sure it wasn't us.
   b) Nobody knows when it will end.
   c) It was wrong from the start, wasn't it?

5 a) Well, things can go wrong in any business.
   b) We didn't mix up anything.
   c) You can't justify a mix-up.

6 a) I'll keep in touch.
   b) Looking forward to your questions.
   c) Thanks, I'll do that.

TAKING ACTION

B **Complete Speaker B's part, apologising first and then promising to take action.**

1 A: We haven't received your new catalogue yet.   *send*
   B: I'm sorry about that. *I'll have it sent to you at once.*

2 A: I'm afraid these figures aren't correct.   *check*
   B: I'm terribly sorry. *I'll have them checked for you straightaway.*

3 A: My projector is on the blink again, it seems.   *mend*
   B: I'm sorry. We'll ....

4 A: We got stuck in the lift.   *service*
   B: Oh! Sorry about that. We'll ....

5 A: The spare parts we ordered haven't materialised yet.   *despatch*
   B: I'm awfully sorry. I'll ....

6 A: What about the report you promised a week ago?   *forward*
   B: Sorry. I'll ....

🔊 **70 Listen and practise each model answer after you hear it.**

UNIT 11 | Crisis management

SOUND WORK

INDIVIDUAL SOUNDS

A ◀)) **71 Listen and add the missing consonants in the words below.**

1	port	_port	
2	kill	_kill	
3	range	_ _range	
4	roll	_ _roll	
5	rip	_rip	_ _rip
6	rain	_rain	_ _rain
7	lay	_lay	
8	ream	_ream	_ _ream

◀)) **71 Now listen again and practise the words in sequence. Pay particular attention to the consonant groups.**

What's the rule?

Many words have groups of two or three consonants. When you say those words, do **not** put a vowel sound before or between the consonants.

CONNECTED SPEECH

B ◀)) **72 Listen and complete these noun phrases.**

1 the ..*lines*.. of communication   4 a .... of progress

2 a .... of trouble   5 a .... of advice

3 a .... of confidence   6 a .... of resources

What's the rule?

When a preposition such as *of* (or *from*, *at*, *for*) occurs between other words, the weak form is usually used. So, for instance, *of* becomes /əv/.

◀)) **72 Listen again and practise saying the phrases. Pay particular attention to the weak form /əv/.**

C ◀)) **73 Listen and complete these short conditional sentences. Use the contracted forms.**

1	.... *We could've* .... announced it.	/ˈkʊdəv/
2	.... risked it.	/ˈwʊdəntəv/
3	...................................., if I were you.	/aɪdəˈgriː ɪˌfaɪwəˈjʊː/
4	Suppose	/jʊːdədˈmɪtədˈɪt/
5	.... exploded.	/ˈmaɪtəv/
6	...................................., wouldn't you?	/jʊːdəvˈsaɪndɪt/

In each sentence, underline the words which are transcribed in the right hand column.

◀)) **73 Now listen again and practise the sentences, paying special attention to the contractions underlined.**

ASKING PROBING QUESTIONS

A 🔊 **74 Listen to these two questions. Which one is likely to elicit a more detailed response?**

1 What don't you like about our new safety regulations?

2 What specifically do you not like about our new safety regulations?

Probably question 2, as the word *specifically* will force the speaker to provide more detail.

> **Tip**
>
> Using words like *specifically*, *exactly*, *just*, *in detail*, may help elicit a more specific response as well as more details about the claims being made.

B **Use some of the words in the tip above to make the following questions more probing.**

1 When did you inform the public?

2 When did you recall the product?

3 What caused the food to get contaminated?

4 How much money did you allocate for the crisis?

5 How is this crisis likely to affect your hygiene and safety regulations?

6 How do you plan to avoid such problems in the future?

🔊 **75 Listen to the sample answers and practise the questions.**

ASKING CHALLENGING QUESTIONS

C **Generalisations like *We always/never do it like that, Everyone/No one does it like that,* or *We must/should/can't do it like that,* etc. tend to stop the discussion. There are times when it can be very useful to challenge such bold assertions.**

🔊 **76 Listen to how this can be done.**

1 A: Our employees are not interested in first aid training.

B: What evidence do you have for that statement?

2 A: We must not let the media know about this incident.

B: What would happen if we did?

D **Challenge the following statements.**

1 A: Everyone thinks fire drills are a waste of time.

B: ....?

2 A: There has never been an accident on our premises.

B: ....?

3 A: I must finish this report by Tuesday.

B: ....?

4 A: Disaster simulations are very expensive to conduct.

B: ....?

5 A: All our customers are pleased with the information we provide.

B: ....?

6 A: A report like that is just not good enough.

B: ....?

🔊 **77 Listen to the sample answers and complete B's part. Then listen again and practise B's responses.**

SURVIVAL BUSINESS ENGLISH

SOUND WORK

INDIVIDUAL SOUNDS

A Circle the word with a different vowel sound in each set.

1	stake	ret**ai**l	**a**lliance	takeover
2	**ear**nings	merger	conf**ir**m	disapp**ear**
3	man**a**ge	advant**a**ge	profit	eng**a**ged
4	b**uy**out	amb**i**tious	host**i**le	acqu**i**re
5	retailer	create	p**ay**ment	for**ei**gn
6	loan	perf**or**m	b**oar**d	launch

◀)) **78** Listen to check your answers. Check with the key. Then listen again and practise saying the words.

CONNECTED SPEECH

B ◀)) **79** Listen to the recording and complete these sentences about the future with the words you hear.

1 The next meeting ...*won't be*... until March.

2 It .... boost our presence in Asia.

3 Analysts are forecasting that their broadband business .... 50,000 new customers by the end of the year.

4 There are rumours that the French .... ask for EU funds to bolster their ailing car industry.

5 Is it true they .... a new agreement?

6 Sandra .... time to come to the board meeting.

7 We expect this programme to take off in March or April when project offices .... established.

◀)) **79** Now listen again and practise saying the sentences.

C ◀)) **80** Listen to these sentences and practise the contractions in the future forms.

STRESS AND INTONATION

D Put the following wordsw into two groups according to their stress pattern.

~~advantage~~   ~~company~~   management   alliance   objectives

position   suitable   takeover   shareholders   successful

Ooo	oOo
company	*advantage*
....	....
....	....
....	....
....	....

◀)) **81** Listen to the recording and check your answers.

NUMBERS

A Read these figures out loud.

a) 14   b) 40   c) 7.52   d) 53%   e) 2/3

f) 211   g) 3,456   h) €567,096   i) £123m

◀)) **82 Listen and practise saying the figures.**

B ◀)) **83 Listen and complete the text.**

Orion Technology Partners yesterday announced plans to buy Rowland Consulting, a rival pan-European e-business consultancy, for $....................[1]m in cash and shares.
A windfall of $ ....[2]m in cash will be shared by Rowland's ....[3] partners, who founded the Vienna-based business in ....[4]. The remaining payment comes in the form of about ....[5]m shares and options for shares.

Rowland's partner group is expected to receive ....[6]m options vested over ....[7] years, while its employees will get ....[8]m options vested over ....[9] years.

C The chairwoman of Astral Power plc, a large independent power producer, is presenting the interim results for the first half year.

◀)) **84 Listen to the first part of her presentation and correct the six mistakes in the table below.**

Financial Summary			
	6 months to ~~13~~ 30 June	previous 6 months	Change
Turnover Gross Net	 £417m £121m	 £311m £98m	 +41% +23%
PBIT (Profit before interest and tax)	£72m	£75m	-26%
Earnings per share	29p	1.8p	+61%

D Complete the second part of the presentation with linking words and phrases from the box.

As you all know	In addition	First
I'd now like to turn to	Secondly	~~Moving on to the area of~~

..Moving on to the area of..[1] growth, I am very pleased with the progress we are making in forging a new corporate culture worldwide, particularly in Europe and North Africa. ....[2], in Europe, we completed the acquisition of GenElex's 24.6% interest in the Gyula power station in Hungary. This purchase increases Astral Power's ownership in Gyula to 93.7%, and strengthens our position as one of Central and Eastern Europe's leading independent power generators.
....................[3], in Morocco, we acquired EnerJebel at a cost of £5m, while Essaouira, in which we have 35% ownership interest, is studying new opportunities arising from mergers and other changes in the market.
....................[4] the outlook. We expect that trading in the next quarter will be similar to the pattern reflected in the interim results for the period ending 30 June. ....[5], we continue to anticipate a step-up in turnover and earnings next year, particularly as a result of new successful acquisitions.
....................[6], we remain committed to delivering shareholder value and maintaining the highest standards of professionalism.

◀)) **85 Listen and check your answers.**

SURVIVAL BUSINESS ENGLISH

Answer key

LANGUAGE WORK

1 Communication

Vocabulary

A

2 c 3 a 4 b 5 c 6 c 7 a

B

2 c 3 e 4 a 5 d 6 b

C

1	tell	6	tell
2	tell	7	say
3	tell	8	tell
4	say	9	say
5	tell	10	say

D

1 tell
2 say
3 told
4 tell
5 say
6 told

Language review

A

2 bush
3 purposes
4 grapevine
5 end... stick
6 head... tail
7 brick wall

B

1 to keep someone in the loop
2 to get it straight from the horse's mouth
3 to come straight to the point
4 to put somebody in the picture
5 to be on the same wavelength

C

2 get straight to the point
3 kept in the loop
4 got it straight from the horse's mouth
5 are on the same wavelength

D

2 b 3 e 4 a 5 d

E

2 was at a loss for words
3 give me the low-down
4 air their views
5 dropped a hint

Writing

A

The words in italics are used to
c) contrast ideas.

B

Sentences **1**, **4** and **5** use linkers correctly.

C Sample answers

2 Even though the talk was extremely interesting, I left the room after a couple of minutes.
or
Even though the talk was awfully boring, I sat through it.
3 Despite the fact that he knew he was wrong, he refused to admit it.
6 I felt alert throughout the meeting in spite of my tiredness.
or
I felt sleepy throughout the meeting because of my tiredness.

D

1 to beat about the bush = to delay talking about the most important part of a subject
2 bearish = the stock market is said to be bearish when prices are expected to fall, and people sell a lot of shares as a result
3 to waffle = to talk a lot without making any clear or important points
4 a flop = a failure
5 scarcity = if there is a scarcity of something, there is not enough of it

E Sample answer

> To: L. Taite, Head of HR
> Subject: Communication skills training course
>
> Dear Mr Taite,
> I should like to attend a Communication & People Skills course organised by our local college. The course is from 7 to 13 October and the fee is £650.
> I believe this seminar would contribute enormously to my professional development and would ultimately benefit the whole department, as the main focus is on interpersonal skills.
> I would be very grateful if you could enable me to get financial support from our Staff Development Scheme.
> Thank you for considering my request.
> With best wishes,
> [your name or initials]

2 International marketing

Vocabulary

A

2 marketing strategy
3 product portfolio
4 brand identity
5 market segmentation
6 customer retention

B

2 b 3 d 4 a 5 b 6 c 7 b 8 d

Language review

A

2 steadily improving balance sheet
3 ambitious market research programme
4 new public relations department
5 extremely impressive profit figures
6 rapidly expanding overseas operations

B

2 marketing
3 trade
4 advertising
5 brand
6 sales

Writing

A

2 Their mailing list contains plentiful information and data so that they won't have any difficulty identifying the most appropriate recipients for the mailshots.
3 Their competitors, however, still have to go through a specialist direct mail agency in order to reach potential customers, which costs them extra time and money.
4 Every company must work hard in order to compete or even survive.
5 The government decided to introduce a quota with a view to limiting exports of textile products from India.
6 They increased their competitiveness so that their market share would increase.

B

The three linkers in exercise A are used to
c) express the purpose of something.

C

3 it   4 a   5 fact   6 lot   7 ✓   8 in   9 ✓   10 them
11 a   12 ✓

D

2 considering
3 enclose
4 arrange
5 require
6 contact

E Sample answer

To: Igor Cutka
Cc:
Bcc:
Subject: CEIMD brochure and poster
Dear Mr Cutka
With reference to Professor Trollerova's letter of 20 June, I would like to request an extra 5 copies of both your new brochure and poster. Please address them to:

Mr Ivan Gasperlin, Manager,
Kommerz Bankm, Trubarjeva 47
1000 Ljubljana, Slovenia
Thank you in advance.

Best wishes
Ivan Gasperlin

3 Building relationships

Vocabulary

A

1 B: Yeah. They've certainly managed to *build up* a good business over the years.
2 B: Absolutely. There's nothing like trade to *strengthen* relations.
3 B: Yes. That's great. *Restoring* relations is probably the best decision they could make.
4 B: Definitely. We need to find ways to *foster* cooperation.
5 B: I agree. I think it's really *undermining* future cooperation.
6 B: To be honest, I wonder what took them so long to *sever* relations with such an unreliable distributor.

B

2 c   3 c   4 a   5 b   6 a

Language review

A

2 f   3 h   4 g   5 c   6 b   7 a   8 e

B

2 looking forward to
3 turned ... round
4 meet up
5 worked out
6 went over
7 carried on
8 checking in
9 turned up
10 goes back

Writing

A

a), b) and c) are true.

B

2 a   3 a   4 c   5 c   6 b

C

2 their *not* there
3 try *not* tried
4 to *not* for
5 talk *not* talking
6 equipment *not* equipments
7 creating *not* create
8 with *not* for

D

~~The company runs other funds that would have competed with the joint venture.~~

Sample answer

Futuro Office
98 Artillery Lane
Harefield, Uxbridge
Middlesex UB7 5LS

MORRISON OFFICE
SUPPLIES INTERNATIONAL

1 Connaught Place, Edinburgh EH2 7EY

5 October

Dear Mr Lindsey,

Thank you for your letter of 21 September.

We would indeed welcome further details of your 'Avalon' seminar chairs, as we have recently received numerous enquiries about alternative office seats.

Could you please specify exactly what discount you are prepared to offer on items from that particular collection?

As regards your website, the new design is astounding. However, we find that the previous version of your online catalogue was easier to browse through. We registered with your site a week ago and hope we will be among the lucky winners.

We would like to take this opportunity to add that, for us, too, it has been a pleasure to do business with you.

We look forward to hearing from you.

Francis Potter, Manager, Futuro Office

4 Success

Vocabulary

2   economic recession
3   annual sales
4   retail outlets
5   turning point
6   buying spree
7   business acumen

B

2   de(regulate)
3   co(-workers)
4   ultra(-efficient)
5   out(performed)
6   ex(-president)
7   under(rating)
8   down(turn)
9   re(locating)
10 mis(judged)

C

2 h **3** f **4** g **5** b **6** a **7** d **8** c

Idioms:

a) are getting there   b) rise to the top
c) does well   d) a success story
e) making a go of   f) bear fruit
g) get results   h) make their mark

Language review

A

2 a **3** b **4** b **5** a **6** a

B

1	2
(2) had censured	(1) has appointed
(3) ordered	(2) was announced
(4) agreed	(3) owns
(5) have been probing	(4) is seen
	(5) had announced
	(6) was appointed

C

2   've/have left; 've/have checked
3   has been
4   had ... been
5   had ... taken off
6   has given

D

2   has sold
3   said
4   has made
5   wanted
6   has long used
7   was launched
8   has been downloaded
9   include
10 provide
11 had been waiting

Writing

A

2   pay *not* paying
3   assignment *not* assignments
4   to *not* on
5   successful *not* succeed **or** do *not* are
6   cent *not* cents
7   assess *not* assessment
8   than *not* then
9   fewer *not* few

Sample answer

Futuro Office
98 Artillery Lane
Harefield, Uxbridge
Middlesex UB7 5LS

GRAND COMPUTERS
73 Gloucester Road
Leeds LS2 6EQ
Tel 013 223 1314 / Fax 013 223 1415

30 March

Dear Mr Jacobson,

Thank you for your letter of 20 March, as well as for the attached details of your new range of LJP/scanners.

I wish to confirm our order for 12 Nexus 2K PCs and 8 Orion Plus laser-jet printers. However, it seems that a slight error has occurred regarding discounts. As a matter of fact, you had agreed to give us a 3% discount on both the Nexus 2K PC and the Orion Plus LJP, and not just on the former as stated in your letter.

We would be grateful if you could contact us as soon as possible to confirm this formally.

Looking forward to hearing from you soon.

Yours sincerely,

Norma Fury

Norman Furey
Deputy Manager

5 Job satisfaction

Vocabulary

A

2 a **3** d **4** b **5** a **6** a **7** b **8** b **9** c **10** d **11** c

Language review

A

2 were made
3 has ... been revised / was revised
4 is ... being negotiated
5 had been given
6 be used

B **Sample answer**

2 How many people were made redundant last year?
3 Whose leave policy has recently been revised? / was recently revised?
4 What sort of agreement is currently being negotiated?
5 Would Tom have resigned if he had been given a pay rise earlier?
6 When should a tough style of leadership be used?

C **Sample answer**

3 A: Has the conference room been booked?
   B: Yes, it has. It was booked earlier this morning.
4 A: Have the folders and note-pads been ordered?
   B: Yes, they have. We ordered them last week. / They were ordered last week.
5 A: Has the PowerPoint equipment been checked?
   B: Sorry, that still needs to be done. I'll get someone to do that next Monday.
6 A: Has a room for the trainer been booked?
   B: No, I'm afraid that still needs to be done. I'll make sure it's booked by the end of the week.

7 A: Have the local media been informed?
   B: Yes, they have. They were informed earlier this month.
8 A: Has the social evening been planned?
   B: Yes, it has. It was planned at our last meeting, actually.

D

1 B: I know. We're going to *get/have it redecorated* soon.
2 B: Right. In that case, we'd better *get/have it translated* immediately.
3 B: We definitely need to *get/have it fixed*.
4 B: Yes. I think we should *get/have it serviced* without delay.
5 B: Well, why don't you *get/have them/it checked*?

Writing

A

FairerTrade Ltd seeks an Assistant Project Manager for 12 months on this project funded by the Trust Fund for Kazakhstan and administered by the World Bank. The project, which commenced in January this year, aims to improve the capacity of Kazakhstani communities to manage local government structures for the planning and implementation of local development initiatives. Through the project, village-level development councils have been established across the country, through which small-scale grant funds are being channelled.

B

1 be appointed (*or* should be appointed)
2 will be paid
3 are set out
4 will be issued

C **Sample answer**

77 Dunham Road
Bolton, Lancashire BL3 2FK

Ms Karen Poulson
Recruitment Officer
FairerTrade Ltd
Denzell House
5 Connaught Avenue, Congleton
Cheshire CW1 7TL

17 March

Dear Ms Poulson,
Re: Assistant Project Manager, Kazakhstan
Thank you very much for your letter of 14 March, and for the particulars of post attached. I am delighted to have been selected, and would like to confirm that I do wish to take up the post and will be available to start work on April 8.
I enclose a full medical report from Bolton General Hospital.
                    ... ving the contract.

Andrew Harris

Andrew Harris

D

2 a **3** c **4** b **5** b **6** c

E

The six correct linkers in exercise A are used to
b) express the cause of something.

6 Risk

Vocabulary

A

Across
4 weigh up
8 eliminate
10 immediate

Down
1 negligible
2 spread
3 potential
5 huge
6 minuscule
7 gauge
9 remote

B
1 anticipate; foresee
2 encounter; face
3 estimate; measure
4 prioritise; reduce

C
1 Predict   2 Meet   3 Assess   4 Manage

D
2 f   3 a   4 b   5 d   6 c

Language review

A
1 rather
2 exceptionally
3 dramatically
4 steadily
5 sharply
6 slightly
7 fairly
8 gradually
9 badly
10 fully

B
2 ... increase gradually/gradually increase.
3 ... to increase dramatically/dramatically increase with the introduction of their new soft drink.
4 ... grew significantly, reflecting the group's rapid expansion over the last year.
5 ... net profits have risen sharply to €1.14bn.
6 ... microchip shares fell slightly.

Writing

A
The words in *italics* are used to
a) reinforce an idea, add information.

B
2 f   3 a   4 d   5 b   6 c

C
3 they
4 in
5 ✓
6 be
7 a
8 with
9 ✓
10 the

D
1 Paula: I hear someone had a nasty fall in the staff restaurant at lunch time.
2 Jeff: Pretty nasty, yes. You know Jim, don't you?
3 Paula: Jim Perry from Accounts?
4 Jeff: That's right, yes. Well, he slipped somewhere near the salad bar.
5 Paula: Near the salad bar? But how did it happen?
6 Jeff: Apparently, one of our attendants had spilt some oil, and was about to clean up, but too late.
7 Paula: Oh dear. Poor Jim! Is he badly hurt?
8 Jeff: A broken elbow, as well as a minor head injury. At least that's what Mary Dawson diagnosed. She called an ambulance straight away.
9 Paula: Oh yeah. She's got a first-aid certificate, hasn't she? It's really good to have someone like her around.
10 Jeff: Absolutely. We need people like her. Besides, we must also make sure canteen users are properly warned of wet or greasy surfaces.

E Sample answer

Jim Perry was badly injured today at lunch time when he fell after slipping on a greasy surface on his way to the salad bar. As it turned out, one of our attendants had just spilt some oil and was just about to clean up, but apparently did not do so quickly enough.

Mary Dawson was there and saw what happened. She has a first-aid certificate and immediately diagnosed a broken elbow as well as a minor head injury. An ambulance was called, and Mr Perry was taken to hospital.

7 Management styles

Vocabulary

A

D	I	R	E	C	T	I	V	E						C
E	R		M											E
C	A		P					F						N
I	T	S	O	C	I	A	B	L	E					T
S	I		W					E						R
I	O		E					X						A
V	N		R		L	O	G	I	C	A	L			L
E	A		I					B						I
	L		N					L						S
	O	R	G	A	N	I	S	E	D					I
A	U	T	O	C	R	A	T	I	C					N
	I	N	S	P	I	R	I	N	G					G

B
2 competence / incompetent
3 loyal / disloyal
4 considerate / consideration
5 irresponsible / responsibility
6 indecisive / decisiveness

C
2 competence
3 loyal
4 consideration
5 irresponsible
6 decisive

D
2 b   3 d   4 a   5 b   6 d   7 c   8 a   9 a

Language review

A
1 it
2 the latter
3 they; this
4 (the) one; their
5 then
6 theirs

B

Text 1

2 *their* = multinational companies

3 *which* = middle management ranks

4 *they* = Women in the United States

5 *the question* = Is it possible that they are ignoring the potential within their own ranks?

6 *Its* = A US organisation

7 *their* = women('s)

8 *them* = women

Text 2

1 *them* = global companies

2 *their* = global companies(')

3 *we* = our firm / a leading recruitment and management consultancy

4 *them* = someone

5 *they* = someone

6 *they* = someone

7 *it* = being good socially

8 *that* = the fact that the question whether leaders are born or made is elusive

9 *their* = companies(')

10 *it* = the answer to the question whether leaders are born or made

Writing

A

2 c 3 a 4 a 5 b 6 b

B

The six correct linkers in exercise A are used to

c) express the cause or the result of something.

C

~~Good management looks after its existing clientele superbly and goes after markets offering the largest sales.~~

D Sample answer

Dear Mr Fekete,

Thank you for your letter of 30 August. We are very pleased to have been recommended, and to accept your extremely interesting proposal. The Vernon Morgan College of English was founded 20 years ago in order to provide executives from all over the world with very high quality tailor-made language training in an area of Britain which has an international reputation for academic excellence.

Within our centre, we provide highly qualified, enthusiastic and professional trainers and consultants who are dedicated to the success of our clients.

We can provide consultants with considerable experience in your field as some of our best clients include AGROCHEM (Milan) and Petrosur (Valencia), for whom we have provided executive language training for over five years.

Our centre also offers a full social programme which gives each individual the opportunity to mix with local business people and integrate with the local community.

The enclosed copy of our new prospectus details the various executive language training programmes, as well as the range of accommodation available.

We would be pleased to grant you a special discount of 20% on all course fees quoted in the brochure for the first group of executives you send us and 12% on all subsequent groups of ten or more participants. We look forward to your reply and to a fruitful relationship.

Best wishes,

Jessica Dunstone, Principal

8 Team building

Vocabulary

A

1 impolite

2 irrelevant

3 intolerant

4 immature

5 illegible

6 inexperienced

7 unimaginative

8 unenthusiastic

9 impractical

10 inefficient

The two adjectives which cannot be used to describe someone's character are *irrelevant* and *illegible*.

B

2 miserable

3 biased

4 renowned

5 premium

6 irritable

C

2 mismanagement

3 disincentive

4 irreversible

5 realign

6 bimonthly

D

2 give and take

4 touch and go

E

2 peace and quiet

3 supply and demand

4 trial and error

5 stocks and shares

6 rules and regulations

Language review

A

2 b 3 c 4 a 5 a

B

2 a2 b1 3 a2 b1 4 a1 b2 5 a1 b2

Writing

A

2 e 3 d 4 a 5 f 6 c

B

1 time relations

2 present; future

C Sample answer

The comments made by sales staff revolve around three areas: (a) lack of punctuality, (b) behaviour in meetings and (c) tactlessness, especially with female colleagues.

(a) at least two people resent the fact that Alan is often late for meetings; he was accused of using the time to make more calls;

(b) a number of people obviously dislike what they call his 'arrogance' in meetings; they feel put down by his interventions and find it difficult to put forward their ideas;

(c) his racist and sexist comments have a demoralising effect on everyone.

9 Raising finance

Vocabulary

A

2 cash flow
3 instalments
4 stake
5 administration
6 grants
7 principal
8 overdraft
9 assets
10 mortgage
11 bankruptcy
12 business angel

B

2 a   3 b   4 c   5 c   6 a   7 b   8 c   9 a

Language review

A

2 ... growing market *for* high-speed internet access.
3 ... involved *in* the deal ...; ... the complexity *of* the issue.
4 ... to blame *for* the downfall *of* the company.
5 ... had thrived *on* rising property prices ...
6 Public protests *about* the cost ...; ... worries *about* the impact *on* business and inflation ...

B

1	into	7	in
2	of	8	at
3	for	9	on
4	on	10	from
5	on	11	in
6	for	12	with

C

2 The engineering company KNG first hinted *at* a share buyback last month.
3 Such buybacks are rarely implemented, although many companies have sought permission *for* them.
4 The CEO said the company would concentrate *on* medium-sized acquisitions.
5 KNG's international division accounts *for* just 23% of sales.
6 Several governments insisted *on* creating specific safeguard rules allowing them to block Chinese imports.

Writing

A

2 a   3 d   4 f   5 c   6 b

B

A special word order is used in the six sentences in exercise A in order to **b)** add emphasis

C

3	✓	10	of
4	and	11	✓
5	an	12	the
6	✓	13	may
7	of	14	any
8	even	15	✓
9	✓		

D

2	remind	5	arrange
3	have ... had	6	made
4	assume		

E Sample answer

Dear Mr Lekic,
Thank you for your fax of 30 November.
We are aware that invoice no. GDB\00\06 is still outstanding. As a matter of fact, only part of the goods have arrived to date, and we are still waiting for item PG-34A to be delivered.
Could you look into this matter promptly as it is essential that we get the stock in before the festive season starts.
Full payment will be made as soon as we receive all the goods.
Yours sincerely,

G. Debacke

G. Debacker

10 Customer service

Vocabulary

A

2 c   3 c   4 d   5 a   6 b   7 d   8 d   9 a   10 b

B Sample answers

2 get straight to the point
3 pass the buck
4 ripping people off
5 get to the bottom of the problem
6 the last straw
7 talking at cross purposes
8 going the extra mile

Language review

A

2	working	5	being
3	ignoring	6	taking
4	letting		

B

2 ... spending a lot of money on training.
3 ... complaining about our prices.
4 ... overcharging us / having overcharged us.
5 ... promising too much to the customer.
6 ... not taking / not having taken the customer feedback seriously enough.

An infinitive could be used instead of a gerund in sentence 3.

C

2	opting	5	to structure / structuring
3	to provide	6	Billing
4	to ensure / ensuring	7	having

Writing

A

3	if	7	will	11	or
4	✓	8	for	12	as
5	and	9	a	13	it
6	✓	10	must	14	✓

B Sample answers

Complaint about delivery: **5 / 7 / 6 / 4 / 2 / 9**

Reply to a reminder to pay: **11 / 1 / 3 / 8 / 10**

C

2	under	**4**	for	**6**	to
3	for	**5**	in	**7**	with

D Sample answer

Thank you for your letter concerning our reminder to settle invoice no. TB/245/c.

Please accept our apologies for indeed sending you this reminder by mistake.

Upon checking our records, we realised that an invoice meant for another customer bears a very similar reference number, hence the confusion.

We would like to thank your for the prompt settlement of the above invoice, and will do our utmost to avoid such mistakes in the future.

We are sorry for the inconvenience caused and look forward to doing further business with you.

Unit 11 Crisis management

Vocabulary

A

Across

1 Safety
2 care
3 action
4 take
5 damage
7 loss
9 release
10 flow

Down

1 speed
2 contingency
3 admission
6 press
8 legal

B

3	leader	**7**	interest	**11**	action
4	crisis	**8**	percentage	**12**	managers
5	fear	**9**	decision	**13**	range
6	stress	**10**	expertise		

Language review

A Sample answers

2 If they hadn't recalled the faulty cars immediately, some serious accidents might have happened.

3 If they had listened to their customers' comments and suggestions, they would have been able to improve their services.

4 If we hadn't got rid of all our older machines, we wouldn't have an excellent safety record.

5 If we hadn't invested so much in safety equipment, the number of shopfloor injuries wouldn't have dropped by half.

6 If they had had a contingency plan, they wouldn't have been unable to act / would have been able to act.

B

2	No matter	**5**	Whatever
3	otherwise	**6**	however much
4	unless		

Writing

A

2	Yet	**6**	Thirdly
3	Firstly	**7**	As a result
4	Secondly	**8**	Finally
5	even	**9**	even

B

2 resist *not* resisting
3 cooperative *not* cooperatively
4 fill *not* feel
5 affected *not* affect
6 their *not* theirs
7 need *not* needed
8 issues *not* issue
9 with *not* over
10 company's *not* company
11 be *not* have

C Sample answers

We are writing in connection with the Delux Cool & Heat-4000 air-conditioning system we purchased on 5 September and which was installed by one of your engineers two days later.

Yesterday evening, one of the indoor units caught fire. The fire spread quickly, causing extensive damage to one of our offices.

Although the surveyors have not produced their final report yet, they seemed positive that the fire was caused by a faulty component rather than by careless installation.

In our interest as well as in yours, we recommend that you have all indoor units in that series thoroughly inspected, starting with ours.

We would also be grateful if you could supply a replacement unit as soon as possible.

We look forward to hearing from you.

D Sample answers

Dear Mr Edgerton

We are very sorry to hear you have experienced a serious problem with one of our products.

We would like to point out that we have sold and installed over 200 Delux Cool & Heat-4000 air conditioning systems over the past three years, and that we have never had a single complaint before.

It may well be that the operating instructions were not followed properly. However, we have also made contact with the manufacturer and asked them to inspect that particular series of indoor units.

Meanwhile, a replacement unit is on its way to you, and one of our engineers will contact you soon. We trust the exact cause of the problem will be determined shortly.

We look forward to doing further business with you.

Yours sincerely,

12 Mergers & acquisitions

Vocabulary

A

1 launched
2 taken
3 set up
4 approved
5 rejected
6 sold

B

2 a **3** d **4** a **5** b **6** c **7** c **8** d **9** a **10** c

Language review

A

100%   1   3   2   5   4   100**%** sure
sure won't ←————————————————→   will happen
happen

B

1 will probably benefit
2 no chance of the merger
3 are bound to worry
4 definitely won't increase
5 is certain to become/be
6 I doubt whether
7 unlikely to bid

Writing

A

3 ✓
4 down
5 up
6 it
7 an
8 a
9 their
10 ✓
11 very
12 over
13 the
14 and

B

2 at **3** at **4** from **5** in **6** at

C

1 c **2** d **3** e **4** b **5** a

TALK BUSINESS

Introduction

Vowels					
/ɒ/		/e/		/ɑ:/	
1	job	**1**	sell	**1**	card
2	knowledge	**2**	friendship	**2**	heart
3	want	**3**	said	**3**	laugh
/eɪ/		/eə/		/ɑɪ/	
1	pay	**1**	share	**1**	price
2	break	**2**	chair	**2**	buyer
3	train	**3**	their	**3**	height
Consonants					
/ʃ/		/s/		/j/	
1	option	**1**	sell	**1**	year
2	conscious	**2**	proceed	**2**	Europe
3	insurance	**3**	scientific	**3**	million

1 Communication

Sound work

B

	/ɪ/	/iː/
1	minutes	
2		speech
3		these
4	business	
5	stick	
6		deal
7	inhibited	
8		least

C

1 6 **2** 7 **3** 10 **4** 12

E

a) up   **b)** down

Survival business English

A *See audio script* 6.

B

ROMA KITCHENS

To: Paula Vecchi
Ron Hornby called. Company: Furniture World
Day: Tues Time: 10.45
S/HE:
• wants you to phone back on: 020 8543 3553
• left this message: when can you meet him at the Trade Fair next week?

Standard ☐   Urgent ✓   He's in all afternoon till 5.30.

C

2 a **3** b **4** e **5** c

2 International marketing

Sound work

B

/ɒ/	/ʌ/	/əʊ/
offer	income	wholesaler
profit	government	overseas
/ɔ:/	/ə/	/uː/
report	political	move
brainstorm	developing	too

C *See audio script* 9.

E *See audio script* 11.

Survival business English

A

6 4 1 7 2 5 3 8

B

1 prepare in advance / prepare beforehand
2 crazy ideas / cranky ideas
3 at the beginning / at the outset
4 rules to follow / rules to respect
5 ideas put forward / ideas proposed

NB: In this context, the words and phrases used in the recording *mean the same* as those in the script.

C

1 d   2 a   3 e   4 b   5 c   6 e   7 d   8 a   9 c   10 b

3 Building relationships

Sound work

A *See audio script 14.*

B *See audio script 15.*

D *See audio script 17.*

Survival business English

A

The conversation is rather unsuccessful. Speaker A tries hard to establish some common ground with Speaker B. The latter, however, does not sound interested and gives mostly one-word answers.

B *See audio script 19.*

C *See audio script 20.*

4 Success

Sound work

A

1 recognised (ends in /d/, the others end in /ɪd/)
2 introduced (ends in /t/, the others end in /d/)
3 wanted (ends in /ɪd/, the others end in /t/)
4 underestimated (ends in /ɪd/, the others end in /d/)

C

2 watched 1	6 co-authored 3
3 researched 2	7 staffed 1
4 respected 3	8 mismanaged 3
5 misjudged 2	

D

1 40   2 4   3 500   4 two   5 75

Survival business English

A

One-word answers often sound unfriendly and sometimes even rude. In order to respond politely or enable the conversation to develop, a follow-up comment is often necessary.

B *See audio script 26.*

C

b) 2   c) 6   d) 5   e) 4   f) 3

D *See audio script 27 for sample answers.*

E

Such comments would generally be perceived as too direct, or even downright rude or aggressive.
See audio script 28.

5 Job satisfaction

Sound work

A

2 They've *(have) been* asked to work overtime.
3 They'd *(had) been* trained to work under pressure.
4 Some of them *were* forced to choose between work and home.
5 A decent balance between work and personal life *was* rated very highly.

B

Oo	oO	Ooo	oOo
balance	award	benefits	appraisal
colleague	career	salary	promotion

C *See audio script 31.*

Survival business English

A *See audio script 32.*

B *See audio script 33.*

6 Risk

Sound work

A *See audio script 34.*

C *See audio script 36.*

D

2 a   3 b   4 c   5 b   6 a

Survival business English

A

1 c   2 h   3 d   4 b   5 g

B

strong agreement – c, a, e, f, b, g, d, h – strong disagreement

C *See audio script 39.*

7 Management styles

Sound work

B

/ʃ/ as in option	/ʒ/ as in decision
pressure rational sociable	leisure precision
/tʃ/ as in cheap	**/dʒ/ as in joint**
catchy coach	manager urgent logical

D *See audio script 43.*

E *See audio script 44.*

Survival business English

A

1 d   **2** a   **3** e   **4** c   **5** b   **6** d   **7** c   **8** e   **9** b   **10** a

B

Exemplifying	1 / 8
Returning to a point made earlier	2 / 7 / 11
Referring to visuals or handouts	3 / 5 / 6 / 10
Concluding	4 / 9 / 12

C *See audio script 46.*

8 Team building

Sound work

A *See audio script 47.*

D *See audio script 51.*

Survival business English

A

2 Could
3 Won't
4 I think you should
5 I'd like

B *See audio script 53 for sample answers.*

D

1 d   **2** a   **3** c   **4** b   **5** e

9 Raising finance

Sound work

B *See audio script 57.*

D *See audio script 59.*

E

↗ 2 4 7
↘ 3 5 6 8

Survival business English

A *See audio script 61.*

B

1 a   **2** e   **3** d   **4** b   **5** b   **6** c   **7** d   **8** e   **9** a   **10** c
See audio script 62.

C *See audio script 63.*

10 Customer service

Sound work

B *See audio script 65.*

D *See audio script 67.*

Survival business English

A

2 c   **3** b   **4** a   **5** a   **6** c

B *See audio script 70.*

11 Crisis management

Sound work

A *See audio script 71.*

B *See audio script 72.*

C *See audio script 73.*

Survival business English

B *See audio script 75 for sample answers.*

D *See audio script 77.*

12 Mergers & acquisitions

Sound work

A

1 **a**lliance
2 disapp**ear**
3 eng**a**ged
4 amb**i**tious
5 for**eig**n
6 l**oa**n

B *See audio script 79.*

D *See audio script 81.*

Survival business English

B *See audio script 83.*

C

Financial Summary			
	6 months to 13 30 June	**previous 6 months**	**Change**
Turnover			
Gross	**£417m** 407	**£311m**	**+41%** 31
Net	**£121m**	**£98m**	**+23%**
PBIT	**£72m**	**£75m** 57	**-26%** +
Earnings per share	**29p** 2.9	**1.8p**	**+61%**

D *See audio script 85.*

Audio scripts

1

See page 52.

1 Communication

2

quick fix; clean sheet; big hit; weak team

3

1	minutes	5	stick
2	speech	6	deal
3	these	7	inhibited
4	business	8	least

4

1 We'll discuss it over lunch.
2 I'll get straight to the point.
3 They'll put me in the picture, won't they?
4 I'm afraid we're going to have to let you go.

5

1 Did you manage to have a quick word with her? ↗
2 Why didn't you drop a hint to Ana? ↘
3 Do you like giving presentations? ↗
4 What time is your talk? ↘

6

S = Secretary, C = Caller

S Good morning. Roma Kitchens. How can I help you?
C Hello. I'd like to speak to Paula Vecchi, please.
S Who shall I say is calling?
C Hornby, Ron Hornby of Furniture World.
S Sorry, it's not a very good line. Could you say that again, please?
C Sure. Ron Hornby, of Furniture World
S Just one moment, please, Mr Hornby, I'll just find out if she's back yet.
   ... I'm afraid she isn't in her office. Is there anything I can do for you?
C Well, it's rather urgent. The reason I'm calling is to fix a meeting at the Trade Fair next week. Could you ask her to call me back later today? I'll be in the office till 5.30.
S And I'll take your phone number just in case...
C Sure. That's 020 8543 3553.
S Can I just read that back to you? 020 8543 3553.
C That's correct. Thank you for your help.
S Not at all, Mr Hornby. I'll make sure she gets the message as soon as she's back. Goodbye.
C Goodbye.

2 International marketing

7

product; monetary; clothing; exporter; domestic; improving

8

product; offer; profit
monetary; income; government
clothing; wholesaler; overseas
exporter; report; brainstorm
domestic; political; developing
improving; move; too

9

1 This year's been marked by expanding overseas operations.
2 We've had to cope with an extremely volatile exchange rate.
3 All I can say is that it's been an incredibly successful trade fair.
4 Do you know who's the head of their new public relations department?
5 We're going to launch a highly ambitious market research programme.

10

a growing market; a trade fair; a free sample; a focus group

11

1 an expanding market
2 a sales network
3 a special offer
4 a single market
5 a balance sheet
6 the exchange rate

12

Interviewer:	So, Pat, what exactly is brainstorming, then?
Pat:	Well, it's very simple. A smallish group of people, sometimes from a variety of backgrounds, get together and spontaneously express their thoughts about ways of solving a specific problem.
Interviewer:	Do they prepare beforehand?
Pat:	Preparation often isn't necessary. The thing is, at the brainstorming stage it's not the quality of the ideas that matters, but the quantity.
Interviewer:	So it's okay to come up with cranky ideas?
Pat:	Absolutely! In fact, the wilder they are, the better.
Interviewer:	I suppose there's someone to lead the session, though.
Pat:	Yeah. There's a group leader to state the problem clearly at the outset, and restate it later if necessary, but other than that everyone has equal status in the group.
Interviewer:	Mm. That sounds interesting. Does that mean there are no guidelines to go by?
Pat:	Not quite. In fact, there are rules to respect if the brainstorming is to be successful.
Interviewer:	Such as?
Pat:	Well, for instance, only one person at a time is allowed to speak, and everyone has an equal chance to speak.
Interviewer:	But surely the ideas need to be evaluated?
Pat:	Of course, but that's done in a follow-up meeting.
Interviewer:	Just one more question, then. Is there any interaction at all between the group members?
Pat:	Yes, there is. Quite a lot, in fact. Participants are constantly encouraged to suggest combinations or modifications of ideas proposed by other members.
Interviewer:	A kind of 'cross-fertilisation' I suppose. Well, thanks very much for your time, Pat.

13

Extract 1
M: Maybe this is just another wacky idea of mine.
F: Well, at this stage we want all your ideas, however crazy you think they are.

Extract 2
M: OK! ... Right! ... Please! ... We're about to start!
F: So ... the purpose of the meeting this morning is to discuss ways of adapting our new soft drink for the South American market.

Extract 3
M: I think we need to look for ways to reduce manufacturing costs.
F: You're absolutely right. That should be our priority.

Extract 4
M: Edith. I thought you wanted to say something.
F: Yes. Well, one thing we could do is modify the communications.

Extract 5
M: Let's be radical and change both the product and the communications.
F: Wow! That's the best idea I've heard for a long time.

Extract 6
M: I think it's really worth sponsoring some kind of event.
F: Definitely. That's what our main competitors are doing, and it seems to be working quite well. So yes, I'm with you on that.

Extract 7
M: Erm ... Well ... No. I thought I had an idea, but ...
F: ... Don't hold back, Roger. Just say whatever comes to mind.

Extract 8
M: So what's on the agenda?
F: Well, what we need to achieve today is see what conclusions we can draw from Tom's market research report and then discuss the way forward on the basis of that.

Extract 9
M: I have some good news. We can spend 50,000 euros on press advertising.
F: Fantastic!

Extract 10
M: Any other ideas?
F: I think we could spend more on Internet advertising.

3 Building relationships

14
market; build; manage; women

15
damage; cement; encourage; business; develop; establish

16
How *do you* do?
Where *do you* come from?
Did you have a good trip?
What *do you* do in your spare time?
Would you like me to call a taxi?

17
Did you find somewhere to stay?
How do you like your hotel?
Could you recommend a good restaurant?
Where do you spend your holidays?
Would you like to join us for dinner tomorrow?

Do you have his phone number, by any chance?
What did you talk about?
When would you like to come?

18
A: So, Stanley, what about you? Where do you come from?
B: Canada.
A: Really? Whereabouts in Canada?
B: Alberta.
A: Calgary?
B: No, Edmonton.
A: I spent three months at the University of Calgary a couple of years ago ...
B: Oh, yeah. Calgary.
A: What a great time I had in Sunny Alberta! What line are you in, by the way?
B: Accountancy.

19
A: Sarah, I hear you're from Australia?
B: That's right, yeah. I live in Bendigo, northwest of Melbourne.
A: Melbourne! You must find our weather pretty dismal, then.
B: It's alright. Actually, I didn't expect so much sunshine here. Have you ever been to Australia?
A: No, but I might someday. You see, I'm into alternative sources of energy, and I've heard a lot about Australian research into agricultural technology ...
B: ... That's a rapidly growing area, isn't it?
A: Yes. It certainly is. How about you? Are you in the agrotech business as well?
B: No, no, not at all. I'm an accountant, but I was made redundant last year. So now my brother and I are working on a project together.
A: Mm, that sounds interesting. What sort of project is that?
B: Well, he works as a consultant in the tourist industry, and we both love Australia. And one day we identified a gap in the market ...

20
A: So, Stanley, what about you? Where do you come from?
B: I'm from Canada, actually.
A: Really? Whereabouts in Canada?
B: Edmonton. That's in Alberta, in western Canada.
A: What a coincidence! I spent three months at the University of Calgary a couple of years ago ...
B: A small world, some say. Were you there on a course?
A: That's right, yes. They do an excellent intensive management training course.
B: So I've heard. And how did you like Canada?
A: I really had a great time in sunny Alberta! How about you, by the way? What line are you in?
B: Accountancy. Sounds boring, doesn't it?
A: You certainly don't look bored! What's it like?
B: The work is alright and the atmosphere is absolutely brilliant. We're a smallish company – there're only 30 of us.
A: Nice people?
B: Extremely. And we're all very committed to the company.

4 Success

21

1 interested; motivated; recognised; divided
2 appeared; believed; introduced; changed
3 wanted; worked; finished; assessed
4 renamed; underestimated; devalued; underperformed

22

1 **syllable:** booked; launched; passed
2 **syllables:** travelled; produced; posted
3 **syllables:** decided; outperformed; undercharged

23

1 discussed; 2 watched; 3 researched; 4 respected;
5 misjudged; 6 co-authored; 7 staffed; 8 mismanaged

24

A: OK. That's agreed, then. You'll get everything to us by the end of May.
B: Sorry, no. We said we could deliver by the end of <u>June</u>.
A: Right. So the price we agreed is for your deluxe model.
B: No, that's not quite right. £999 is for our <u>standard</u> model, actually.

25

1 **A:** So you're willing to give us a 12% discount if we buy over 14 vehicles.
   B: That's not quite right, I'm afraid. We were talking about <u>40</u> vehicles.
2 **A:** Right. If we ask you to change the specifications, you'll reduce the discount by 2%.
   B: No, I'm afraid in that case we'd have to reduce it by <u>4</u>%.
3 **A:** That's agreed, then. If we pay an extra £300, you'll give us a five-year warranty.
   B: Sorry, no. That'd be an extra £<u>500</u>, in fact.
4 **A:** So if we pay an extra £300, you'll give us a five-year warranty.
   B: I'm afraid we only give a <u>two</u>-year warranty for that amount.
5 **A:** Are you saying that if we increase our order to 500, you'll lower your price to £55 per item?
   B: Well, no. For orders of that size we could only decrease it to <u>75</u>.

26

a) Oh, thanks very much. That's very kind of you.
b) That's right, yes. Straight down this corridor, last door on your left.
c) Yes, of course. Please go ahead.
d) Yes, it is, isn't it. How about closing that window?
e) I'd really appreciate that. Thank you very much.
f) Yes, I have, actually. This is my third visit.

27

1 **A:** Would you like me to double-check those figures?
   B: Oh, thanks a lot. That's very kind of you.
2 **A:** Could I use the photocopier?
   B: Yes, sure. Just go ahead.
3 **A:** Is Arabic your first language, then?
   B: Yes, it is, actually, although we used to speak French as well.
4 **A:** It's a bit stuffy in here, don't you find?
   B: It is, isn't it? Shall we let some fresh air in?
5 **A:** Would you like us to order a taxi for you?
   B: Oh, thanks very much. I don't really fancy walking in this rain!

28

1 I'm afraid we're not in a position to extend your credit at the moment.
2 Could you give us a discount?
3 If you pay on delivery, we could process your order in a week.
4 I'm sorry, but we cannot possibly consider lowering our price even further.
5 If you order over 100, we can give you 8% discount.
6 I was wondering whether you could alter the specifications.

5 Job satisfaction

29

1 She's been praised for her creativity.
2 They've been asked to work overtime.
3 They'd been trained to work under pressure.
4 Some of them were forced to choose between work and home.
5 A decent balance between work and personal life was rated very highly.

30

Group 1: bonus; balance; colleague
Group 2: success; award; career
Group 3: flexible; benefits; salary
Group 4: fulfilment; appraisal; promotion

31

bonus; career; commission; redundancy; assessment; performance; allowance; complaint

32

RV: Rosalia Valdesi.
PW: Good morning, Ms Valdesi. My name's Paul Whitby. I work for an executive recruitment agency.
RV: Oh yes?
PW: I was given your name by Luis Deltell. I believe you know him quite well.
RV: That's right. Yes. And what is it about?
PW: Mr Deltell suggested I call you. He thought you might be interested in a position that's become vacant at GSP Consulting. It's for a senior financial adviser. Would you like to meet to find out a bit more about the post?
RV: Well, thank you very much for contacting me. But to be honest, I don't think there's any point in us meeting. You see, I'm very happy in my current job, and I'm not thinking of going anywhere else.
PW: Sure, I quite understand. Maybe, then, there's someone you could recommend? Someone I could contact and sound out about the job?
RV: Well, let me see …

33

1 **A:** What's the career structure like where you work?
   B: Well, there are lots of opportunities for promotion, I must say.
2 **A:** What fringe benefits do they offer?
   B: All the usual perks, plus a free mobile phone.
3 **A:** I hear Peter's going to be dismissed.
   B: Who would have thought he would be fired?
4 **A:** Personally, I'd enjoy a little more autonomy.
   B: Yes, I need some independence as well.
5 **A:** It's so demotivating having to deal with bureaucracy, don't you find?
   B: Red tape's a nuisance. I hate it!

6 Risk

34

1 **spl**endid; **spr**ing; **str**aight
2 **spl**it; **spr**ee; **str**ong
3 **Tr**y and **spr**ead the ri**sks**.
4 She was **sl**ightly **cr**itical of our re**cr**uitment **str**ategy.
5 **Str**angely enough, they in**tr**oduced new **tr**ade re**strict**ions.
6 Our company is **str**ugg**l**ing to survive. It is an e**xtr**emely **str**ess**f**ul situation.

35

I quite‿agree.
I don't‿agree.

36

1 That's‿out‿of the question, I'm‿afraid.
2 Well, I couldn't‿agree more.
3 That's not‿at‿all how I see it.
4 I'm‿in complete‿agreement.
5 That's‿absolutely right.
6 Are we all‿agreed‿on this‿issue?
7 Alright then. Let's‿agree to disagree.

37

1 quantify; calculate; encounter
2 develop; minimise; estimate
3 reduce; limit; control
4 terrible; minimal; tremendous
5 remote; serious; increased
6 measure; avoid; assess

38

1 **A:** I think all staff e-mails should be monitored.
   B: Absolutely.
   C: You must be joking! What about our rights to privacy?
2 **A:** And using the phone at work to make personal calls is so disgraceful!
   B: I couldn't agree more. While they're chatting, important calls can't get through.
   C: Well, actually, I'm not sure I agree with that. My son is ill, and alone at home. I simply need to talk to him.
3 **A:** I can't see why we have to stand outside in the cold just because we want a smoke.
   B: That's right. Discrimination, that's what I call it.
   C: I can't go along with that. We simply have to respect the non-smokers, that's all.
4 **A:** I wish there was a decent restaurant or snack bar near the office.
   B: Well, Le Jardin is only a ten-minute walk. I love it. Their vegetarian dishes are fabulous.
   C: Do you think so? The Balti Paradise on the main square is a lot better, if you ask me. They do a great buffet.
5 **A:** Don't you think it would be good to have a coffee machine on each floor?
   B: Well, yeah, but people need to get some work done as well.
   C: I can't agree with that argument. Efficiency is not all about sitting at your desk from 9 to 5, you know. It's also about being happy to be at work.
   A: That's right. Our employees need to interact and to share information in a friendly setting. In the long run, good relationships can only benefit the company.

39

1 Shall we go for a drink?
   Great idea.
2 Would you like to join us for lunch tomorrow?
   I'd love to, but I've got another engagement.
3 I wondered whether you could come to our housewarming party on Saturday?
   I'm afraid I can't. I'm going away for the weekend.
4 What about coming round for a drink Friday after work?
   That would be nice. Thanks.
5 We'd like to invite you to our house after the seminar.
   I'd be delighted.
6 Do you fancy a bite to eat?
   Sorry, I can't. No lunch break for me today!

7 Management styles

40

efficient; measure   passion; vision
cheque; jet   March; large

41

1 pre**ss**ure; ra**ti**onal; so**ci**able
2 lei**s**ure; preci**si**on
3 ca**tch**y; coa**ch**
4 mana**g**er; ur**g**ent; lo**g**ical

42

Allan‿is‿extremely sociable‿and‿always joins‿us for lunch.

43

1 Our‿office manager doesn't‿involve‿us‿in‿any decisions.
2 They encouraged‿us to plan‿everything with‿absolute precision.
3 Of course‿it's‿a high-pressure job, but there's‿a lot‿of prestige‿attached to it.

44

charis<u>mat</u>ic – charis<u>ma</u>
<u>comp</u>etent – <u>comp</u>etence
diplo<u>mat</u>ic – diplo<u>ma</u>cy
<u>flex</u>ible – flexi<u>bil</u>ity
in<u>spir</u>ing – inspi<u>rat</u>ion
<u>soci</u>able – socia<u>bil</u>ity

45

<u>Extract 1</u>
I really need to highlight that the increase in overhead costs over the last year is highly significant.
<u>Extract 2</u>
In my presentation this afternoon, I'll be reviewing our sales performance over the last quarter.
<u>Extract 3</u>
It is too early to say how exactly these changes will affect our subsidiaries, but there is no doubt that one consequence will be tighter monitoring of their operations.
<u>Extract 4</u>
Now that we've looked at the main issues, I'd like to consider some possible solutions.
<u>Extract 5</u>
Now, if you think the answer is 'yes', can you just raise your hands?
<u>Extract 6</u>
Once again I'd like to stress the importance of involving staff in the decision-making process.

Extract 7
Right. Let's move on now to the issue of foreign investment.
Extract 8
So, what this means for our company is that some restructuring seems inevitable.
Extract 9
Suppose the competition launches a similar product before you. How would you deal with this?
Extract 10
What I'd like to do today is to present a new appraisal procedure.

46

What I'd like to do at this stage is say a few words about e-mail etiquette, or 'Netiquette', as we sometimes call it. What is it? Well, e-mail etiquette is simply a set of rules for behaving properly in cyberspace.
What kind of rules are there? <u>Let me give you an example</u>. Take quality. The quality of your writing obviously matters to our customers, so we need to make sure we check our grammar and our spelling. In that respect, e-mail is similar to traditional mail.
Now <u>if you look at the slide</u>, you can see "3 Cs". They stand for clarity, conciseness and courteousness. <u>As I said in my introduction</u>, lots of users have storage quotas that limit the amount of e-mail they can deal with. So it's particularly important to be brief. <u>For instance</u>, it's often a good idea to deal with only one topic per e-mail.
There are three other rules I'd like to mention. First, if you have to send very big attachments, it's best to check if the addressee is willing and able to receive them. Second, avoid sending a copy to everyone in your address book! Make sure you select the recipients carefully. And finally, remember to include your name – you'd be surprised how many people forget.
<u>So, to sum up</u>. In business, a lot of the things that are true for traditional correspondence are true for e-mail as well. However, there are some …

8 Team building

47
sociable; imaginative; loyal; efficient; popular; tolerant

48
1   We should have encouraged more debate and discussion.
2   The trainer shouldn't have spent so much time on 'difficult people'!
3   Her presence might have boosted the team's performance.
4   We needn't have hurried to the airport. The plane was late.
5   Where's my key? I must have dropped it somewhere.
6   The team would have been stronger without him.

49
1   You might've tried to talk to me first.
2   They must've felt some tension within the team.
3   They would've done it if they'd had more time.
4   The manager could've delegated more work.
5   He shouldn't've ignored tensions within the team.

50
1   **A:** It's not a very imaginative solution.
     B: But it is <u>practical</u>.
2   **A:** It's not a very practical solution.
     B: But it <u>is</u> practical.

51
1   **A:** Is there anything you dislike in your job?
     B: I hate the <u>paperwork</u>.
2   **A:** How do you feel about all the admin stuff?
     B: I <u>hate</u> the paperwork.
3   **A:** Have you registered for the May seminar?
     B: I have signed up for the <u>June</u> one.
4   **A:** Why don't you register for the June seminar?
     B: I <u>have</u> signed up for the June one.
5   **A:** He wasn't a very enthusiastic team leader.
     B: But he was <u>efficient</u>.
6   **A:** Efficiency was certainly not Harry's forte.
     B: But he <u>was</u> efficient.

52
1   It might be quite difficult to make him change his mind.
2   Could you tell me how you feel about it?
3   Won't that solution be a bit difficult to implement?
4   I think you should tell them what your goals are.
5   I'd like to know what you plan to do.

53
1   I think you should try and build on the strengths of the team.
2   Won't it be a bit expensive to send the team on a weekend training course?
3   I would like each employee to have a say.
4   Could you tell me what your main concern is?
5   Won't those changes be perceived as too drastic?
6   It might be quite risky to suggest removing any of the senior team members.

54
1   I think you should talk to each team member individually.
2   I'm sure that if you removed Tom and Amy, the team would be a lot more effective.
3   We need to involve all team members in the decision-making process.
4   The manager should be replaced with one of the senior sales people.
5   Let's send them all on a one-week training course to strengthen team cohesion.

55
1   **A:** I think you should talk to each team member individually.
     B: I'm afraid that's not really feasible. It would take me over a week!
2   **A:** I'm sure that if you removed Tom and Amy, the team would be a lot more effective.
     B: I appreciate your point of view, but I couldn't possibly do that. Everyone would wonder who's going to be sent away next.
3   **A:** We need to involve all team members in the decision-making process.
     B: I see what you mean, but that's not really practical. Nothing would ever get done on time.

4 **A:** The manager should be replaced with one of the senior sales people.

B: I can see why you would want to do this, but I don't think it would work. It would cause a lot of jealousy amongst the staff in other departments.

5 **A:** Let's send them all on a one-week training course to strengthen team cohesion.

B: That sounds very interesting, but I doubt we can afford it. How about a weekend event?

9 Raising finance

56

asset; private; market; stake; talk; mortgage

57

/æ/ as in bad bank: asset; acquisition; finance
/ə/ as in about Canada: private*; account; purchase*
/ɑː/ as in smart card: market; overdraft; grant
/eɪ/ as in play safe: stake; rate; angel
/ɔː/ as in short course: talk; although; instalment
/ɪ/ as in quick fix: mortgage; percentage; encourage
(*) The letter a in private and purchase is sometimes pronounced /ɪ/.

58

1 Everyone expects a return on their investment.
2 The report contained an assessment of the risks facing European investors.

59

The first instalment is due in April.
The company has gone into administration with debts of about eight million euros.
If we are serious about this acquisition, we'll have to put our money where our mouth is.

60

1 Could I make a suggestion? ↗
2 Do you have a reliable backer? ↗
3 Why do you want to take out a loan? ↘
4 Are you willing to renegotiate the loan? ↗
5 What kind of collateral can you offer? ↘
6 What sort of figure did you have in mind? ↘
7 Does that solve the problem? ↗
8 When can you transfer the money? ↘

61

1 Unfortunately, we couldn't invest in your project in its present form.
2 Maybe we should talk about start-up costs first.
3 Could you offer some additional collateral?
4 I'm afraid that's the lowest rate we can offer.
5 Is there any possibility you could bring in another backer?
6 Your interest rate is higher than we were expecting.

62

1 When will you be in a position to repay the overdraft?
2 Let's go over what we've agreed so far, then.
3 Can I comment on that? I think we must look for other sources of finance.
4 Do you have a cash flow problem?
5 Can you repay the loan in four instalments?
6 I'm sorry, but these figures just don't seem to add up.
7 Let me clarify what I've just said. What I meant was, we might be forced to take legal action.

8 Let's recap on the main points before we move on to our other topic.
9 Why can't you bring in another backer?
10 I'm afraid we were hoping for a slightly lower interest rate.

63

1 **A:** Do you think you'll be able to break even in two years?
B: Well, maybe, erm, that really depends on the market.

2 **A:** So exactly how many backers will you be able to find?
B: Can I get back to you on that one?

3 **A:** Will you accept payment by instalments?
B: We'll think about that.

4 **A:** We'd like to know why the overdraft hasn't been repaid yet.
B: I'll look into that.

5 **A:** How much will you need for start-up costs?
B: Well, I don't know really.

6 **A:** So we're all agreed on the collateral, then?
B: Hold on a minute.

10 Customer service

64

policy; task; customer; repair; retain; recall

65

1 customer care
2 company policy
3 peak time
4 clear intentions
5 cash price
6 repair person
7 progress report

66

1 How do you like working in a call centre?
2 Did you mention having worked abroad?
3 Would you mind filling in this form?
4 How do you deal with complaints?
5 Did you take part in any training?

67

1 I'm afraid you sent me the wrong model.
A: I'm sorry. We should have checked your order more carefully. ✓ 　**B:** I'm sorry. We should have checked your order more carefully.

2 The books we ordered haven't reached us yet.
A: Sorry. You should've been informed that some of the titles are out of stock. 　**B:** Sorry. You should've been informed that some of the titles are out of stock. ✓

3 Some of the goods were badly damaged.
A: I'm sorry. If you let me have the reference numbers, we'll send replacements at once. 　**B:** I'm sorry. If you let me have the reference numbers, we'll send replacements at once. ✓

4 This delay has really messed up our sales.
A: Something has obviously gone wrong. I'm really sorry for this mistake. ✓ 　**B:** Something has obviously gone wrong. I'm really sorry for this mistake.

5 We've again received a reminder for that invoice which was settled three months ago.
    A: I'm sorry. I'll talk to the **B:** I'm sorry. I'll talk to the person responsible   person responsible straightaway. ✓   straightaway.

6 We still haven't received your invoice.
    A: Sorry about that. I'm **B:** Sorry about that. I'm afraid we must have   afraid we must have sent it to the wrong   sent it to the wrong department. ✓   department.

68
1 A: I'm afraid you sent me the wrong model.
   B: I'm sorry. We should have checked your order more carefully.
2 A: The books we ordered haven't reached us yet.
   B: Sorry. You should've been informed that some of the titles are out of stock.
3 A: Some of the goods were badly damaged.
   B: I'm sorry. If you let me have the reference numbers, we'll send replacements at once.
4 A: This delay has really messed up our sales.
   B: Something has obviously gone wrong. I'm really sorry for this mistake.
5 A: We've again received a reminder for that invoice which was settled three months ago.
   B: I'm sorry. I'll talk to the person responsible straightaway.
6 A: We still haven't received your invoice.
   B: Sorry about that. I'm afraid we must have sent it to the wrong department.

69
1 I'm afraid I have to make a serious complaint.
2 I'll look into the matter for you right away.
3 This delay has had a very bad effect on our production schedule.
4 There's probably been a mistake at our end.
5 Your complaint is wholly justified. Please excuse us for this mix-up.
6 If you have any further questions, don't hesitate to contact us direct.

70
1 A: We haven't received your new catalogue yet.
   B: I'm sorry about that. I'll have it sent to you at once.
2 A: I'm afraid these figures aren't correct.
   B: I'm terribly sorry. I'll have them checked for you straight away.
3 A: My projector is on the blink again, it seems.
   B: I'm sorry. We'll have it mended for you immediately.
4 A: We got stuck in the lift.
   B: Oh! Sorry about that. We'll have it serviced right away.
5 A: The spare parts we ordered haven't materialised yet.
   B: I'm awfully sorry. I'll have them despatched to you at once.
6 A: What about the report you promised a week ago?
   B: Sorry. I'll have it forwarded to you right now.

11 Crisis management

71
1 port; sport
2 kill; skill
3 range; strange
4 roll; scroll
5 rip; trip; strip
6 rain; train; strain
7 lay; play
8 ream; cream; scream

72
1 the lines of communication   **4** a sign of progress
2 a source of trouble   **5** a word of advice
3 a loss of confidence   **6** a lack of resources

73
1 We <u>could've</u> announced it.
2 They <u>wouldn't've</u> risked it.
3 <u>I'd agree, if I were you</u>.
4 Suppose <u>you'd admitted it</u>.
5 It <u>might've</u> exploded.
6 <u>You'd've signed it</u>, wouldn't you?

74
1 What don't you like about our new safety regulations?
2 What specifically do you not like about our new safety regulations?

75
1 Just when did you inform the public?
2 When exactly did you recall the product?
3 What specifically caused the food to get contaminated?
4 How much money exactly did you allocate for the crisis?
5 Could you tell me in detail how this crisis is likely to affect your hygiene and safety regulations?
6 Could you tell me in detail how you plan to avoid such problems in the future?

76
1 A: Our employees are not interested in first aid training.
   B: What evidence do you have for that statement?
2 A: We must not let the media know about this incident.
   B: What would happen if we did?

77
1 A: Everyone thinks fire drills are a waste of time.
   B: Does everyone really think so?
2 A: There has never been an accident on our premises.
   B: Have there ever been any occasions when an accident could have happened?
3 A: I must finish this report by Tuesday.
   B: What would happen if you didn't?
4 A: Disaster simulations are very expensive to conduct.
   B: Are all types of disaster simulations very expensive?
5 A: All our customers are pleased with the information we provide.
   B: What evidence do you have for that statement?
6 A: A report like that is just not good enough.
   B: What would be an acceptable standard?

12 Mergers & acquisitions

78

1	stake	ret**ai**l	**a**lliance	**ta**keover
2	**ear**nings	**me**rger	con**fi**rm	disapp**ear**
3	man**a**ge	advan**ta**ge	**pro**fit	eng**a**ged
4	**bu**yout	amb**i**tious	**ho**stile	acqu**i**re
5	re**tai**ler	cre**ate**	**pay**ment	for**ei**gn
6	lo**a**n	perf**o**rm	b**oa**rd	**lau**nch

79

1 The next meeting won't be until March.
2 It'll boost our presence in Asia.
3 Analysts are forecasting that their broadband business will have signed up 50,000 new customers by the end of the year.
4 There are rumours that the French are about to ask for EU funds to bolster their ailing car industry.
5 Is it true they're going to sign a new agreement?
6 Sandra won't have time to come to the board meeting.
7 We expect this programme to take off in March or April when project offices will have been established.

80

1 We'll do it for you.
2 Nikola's going to resign.
3 They won't be able to sell it.
4 They're about to sell their stake.
5 We're going to make a huge profit.
6 They'll have beaten the competition.
7 We aren't going to change our policy.
8 They won't have finished until next Monday.

81

Column 1: company; management; suitable; takeover; shareholders

Column 2: advantage; alliance; objectives; position; successful

82

14	53%	3,456
40	2/3	€567,096
7.52	211	£123m

83

Orion Technology Partners yesterday announced plans to buy Rowland Consulting, a rival pan-European e-business consultancy, for $640m in cash and shares.

A windfall of $27m in cash will be shared by Rowland's 19 partners, who founded the Vienna-based business in 1999. The remaining payment comes in the form of about 6.8m shares and options for shares. Rowland's partner group is expected to receive 3.1m options vested over three years, while its employees will get 1.1m options vested over two years.

84

I'd like to begin by looking at our financial results. Our interim results are solid and our global growth programme is moving ahead. As you can see from this table, gross turnover for the six months ended 30 June was £407m against 311m last year, and profit before interest and tax was £72m against 57m last year, that is to say up 31% and 26% respectively over the corresponding previous period. Basic and fully diluted earnings per share were 2.9p against 1.8p in the previous period.

85

Moving on to the area of growth, I am very pleased with the progress we are making in forging a new corporate culture worldwide, particularly in Europe and North Africa.

First, in Europe, we completed the acquisition of GenElex's 24.6% interest in the Gyula power station in Hungary. This purchase increases Astral Power's ownership in Gyula to 93.7%, and strengthens our position as one of Central and Eastern Europe's leading independent power generators.

Secondly, in Morocco, we acquired EnerJebel at a cost of £5m, while Essaouira, in which we have 35% ownership interest, is studying new opportunities arising from mergers and other changes in the market.

I'd now like to turn to the outlook. We expect that trading in the next quarter will be similar to the pattern reflected in the interim results for the period ending 30 June.

In addition, we continue to anticipate a step-up in turnover and earnings next year, particularly as a result of new successful acquisitions.

As you all know, we remain committed to delivering shareholder value and maintaining the highest standards of professionalism.